Landeg White (see www. la   h
Wales in 1940 and now lives   t
his professional career teach   t
Indies, Trinidad, 1964-1968,   , 1969-
1972, The University of S....a Leone, 1972-1974, the
University of Zambia, 1974-1979, the University of Kent at
Canterbury, 1979-1980, the University of York, 1980-1997
(where he directed the Centre for Southern African Studies) and
Universidade Aberta, Lisbon, Portugal (1997-2010).

His books include *V.S. Naipaul: a Critical Introduction*
(Macmillan, 1975), *Capitalism & Colonialism in Mozambique: a
Study of Quelimane District* (with Leroy Vail, University of
Minnesota Press, 1980), *Oral Poetry from Africa* (with Jack
Mapanje, Longman 1983), *Magomero: Portrait of an African
Village* (Cambridge University Press, 1987), *Power & the Praise
Poem; Southern African Voices in History* (with Leroy Vail,
University Press of Virginia), and *Bridging the Zambesi: a
Colonial Folly* (Macmillan, 1993).

He has also published nine collections of poetry, viz., *For
Captain Stedman* (Peterloo Poets, 1983), *The View from the
Stockade* (Dangaroo Press, 1991), *Bounty* (Dangaroo Press,
1993). *South* (CEMAR, 1999), *Traveller's Palm* CEMAR, 2002),
Where the Angolans are Playing Football: Selected & New Poems
(Parthian Books, 2003), *Arab Work* (Parthian Books, 2006),
Singing Bass (Parthian Books, 2009), and *Letters from Portugal*
(Kondwani Publications, 2014) along with a novel *Livingstone's
Funeral* (Cinnamon Press, 2010.)

His verse translation of *The Lusíads of Luis Vaz de Camões*
(Oxford World's Classics, 1997, rev. ed., 2001) won the TLS
translation prize for 1998. His verse translation of *The Collected
Lyric Poems of Luís de Camões* was published by Princeton
University Press in 2008, and his *Translating Camões: a
Personal Record* by Universidade Católica in 2012. He reviews
regularly for the *Times Literary Supplement* and occasionally for
the *Guardian* and the *London Review of Books*.

To Alice, John & Martin

Living in the Delta

New and Collected Poems

by
Landeg White

Parthian, Cardigan SA43 1ED
www.parthianbooks.com
© Landeg White 2015
ISBN 978-1-910409-88-6
Cover by Robert Harries
Typeset by Elaine Sharples
Printed and bound by Gomer Press, Llandysul
Published with the financial support of the Welsh Books Council.
British Library Cataloguing in Publication Data
A cataloguing record for this book is available from the British Library.

Contents

2

3

4

1

When Paul Celan Met Heidegger

When Paul Celan met Heidegger
in that Black Forest hut

where the philosopher and nature met
in the manner of soiled centuries,

his question hung in the damp air:
what of Jews and the Gypsies?

Blue-eyed Hitler, vegecologist,
anti-smoker and folklorist,

concentrated all wanderers
and earthed them in his fires.

Such was the poet's right to ask
the philosopher was silenced,

and it echoes whenever a plot's
patrolled, viz., what

of refugees, aliens,
asylum-seekers, Palestinians?

Celan found beautiful sport in the orchid.
I write in praise of the canine hybrid

that claims its space by hoisting
a leg, no matter who planted the lamppost.

Living in the Delta

　　　　Darkness,
a wet tarpaulin weighing
down the mangrove, moulders
to a yellow fog, threadbare at dawn.
The fishermen stir from the fire,
their cigarettes trailing candleflies,
then slither narrow dugouts under
roots pale with oysters into the warm
crocodile waters of the creek.
After all these years of words it is still
discovery, the canopy whitening
over the surf, the silver glimmering beach,
and a medieval sea where pelicans
loom on a sandbank and these fishermen
like the centuries rock patiently
at anchor.
　　　　Noon,
the sand vines blazing
purple and the white-hot sand
whistling to my heels, I found
her in the hollow where a coconut bole
strained at its roots, the palm's shadow
dark as the wreck's charred ribs
on the headland, clasping becalmed
the length of her olive body. She
to whom all metaphors return lay
strange and familiar, the gold
and tawny chevrons shifting only
to her breathing. Swamp, strand, the bayscape
taut as a drum.
　　　　Dusk,
and a walk around the liberated

playground, the swing seats
unchained, the see-saw bending,
the toadstool tables turned. Feverish
in twilight, the estate house
crumbles. The Piper revs for take-off,
cantering down the golf course, barking
Scottie in pursuit. We along the flood
defences saunter to the club. Fires
glisten from the compounds where
shoeless children sing of blood,
their guns of bamboo slung across
bare navels.

    Night,
and the swamp road to *Hotel Chuabo*:
suits, fountains, canned music,
dinner like an airport café, varnish
flaking from the wardrobe door. But
Chuabo, meaning stockade, the town's
peasant name, has an eighth-storey
balcony for drinking. Far above
the masses, over the blacked-out *bairros*,
Russian experts, acrobats from Pyongyang
and we, separately expatriate, shuttered
with glass and the drifting stars,
meditate on the salt-logged coconut,
swamps of water hyacinth, the mouldering
steps at dusk where hippos boom
from the papyrus and the river lurks, waiting
its season, silted in the lifetimes
of some of us ... Each of us
rises in this stockade, far from ambush
and famine, to meet the kindly liberators.
They are correctly bearded and smiling.

Incident at a Poetry Reading

(to the late Eduardo White, *primo*)

In the old walled garden the young poets
have spread laden tables under the mango tree.
We stand reverently in the starving city

eyeing the roast suckling pig, samosas,
fried prawns, chicken with groundnut sauce,
goat piri-piri, wines and beers,

while the speech from the dais about the young
poets' aspirations reaches its peroration
in a *caldeirada* of revolutionary slogans,

and we clap, our hands straining to do
what they do next, reaching out for food
and drink until all the tables are cleared

and we stretch our legs under the mango tree,
a black silence in the glistening sky,
enjoying the young poets' newest poetry.

Eduardo is long-limbed. He bears signs
of his mother's tenderness. His sudden
manhood has tightened like a skin.

His poem is angry. The nation is a neglected
garden rank with rotting fruits. Corruption
and our silence are forfeiting victories.

We watch him touched on the shoulder
by uniformed men. He falters in his reading:
detention without trial has its own prosody.

6

But "talk!" they insist. "You are telling truths,"
and the poem ends wildly with kisses and applause
and the evening in an afterglow of pleasure,

beer bottles clinking in the mango tree's shadow,
talk about language and the international standard,
tiny green mangoes dropping on our bare heads,

while beyond the *bairros* past the airport road
despairing peasants flock to the city for food,
and the siege tightens with mutilation and murder.

The Trick

The week I landed, I couldn't distinguish
face from face, tree from tree. I found
girls too ripe, the flowers over-doing it,
the sunsets vulgarly ostentatious,

and the night sky, in dazzling 3D
with its billion lamps, intimidated.
How could I read such over-statement
when irony withered on the tongue?

Beissel described priapic breadfruit,
hibiscus with their flies undone. Witty,
of course, but false. The trick
was never to adumbrate the exotic,

but to be re-born, writing as though
such miracles were entirely natural,
the scheme of things. As began to happen
when faces cracked into separate smiles.

A Sunrise

Dawn hung like dripping sailcloth
over the plumed reeds and papyrus. Tiny
crocodiles as I came in deck plopped
overboard and dissolved. Mosquitoes

drifted like an English drizzle. The barge
swivelled, scouring a bend into a gold
column on the sliding eddies. Then
heat whipped all colours into hiding.

Three days we chugged between countries
emblematically left and right, though the women
gesturing port and starboard their satiric
invitations wore the same embossed bras

and the houses sprouting like grey mushrooms
in the hut-high millet were identical.
Traveller's tales. The girl relaxed in the stern
reading Austen's *Orgulho e Preconceito*.

Afternoons, Mozambique

Senhor Santos is forty-four.
He came with the army and stayed on;
now he owns a store,

a corrugated iron
roof and pink bulging walls
with Santos in vermilion.

From time to time he sells
dried fish, cokes,
a piece of cloth, olive oil.

The floor is cluttered with flour sacks
and boxes of sardines.
The trapped heat is like smoke.

Every windless afternoon
he sleeps on the veranda
by the sewing machines

– Senhor Santos, the tailors,
the clerk who does his letters,
his houseboys, the *ronda*,

and his brown daughters,
pretty in curlers, patiently
watching the road, awaiting

only an event.
Catfish, curled like tobacco,
are drying on a bench.

A limping mongrel licks
its yellow balls.
Sometimes the yard re-echoes

to a jeepful of soldiers
yelling out of their dust storm.
It settles on the hibiscus flowers.

Senhor Santos has long sideburns
and a straw hat:
his trouser leg is torn.

One glittering, domed night
he will wake to AK47s:
he will lose his yard of freedom:

he will mourn these vacant African afternoons.

Cave Paintings

Mwandiona pe, the Shona name, *from where
did you see me?* assumes the vanished
bushmen are playing hide and seek.
On that bald dome of gneiss balancing

impossible boulders four high on its forehead,
much could be believed. We climbed
higher and saw springbok and impala
leaping across the cave wall like a movie,

and a shambling elephant, and buffaloes
keening the air, for all the skill
of the stick-figure hunters, poised.
As we descended, the chartered valley

creased by its turquoise river seemed empty
– though not to Dambushawa, who knew
from every crack and dry water course
playful spirits peered and were chuckling.

Tickling the Censors

Jack's was about a butterfly bar girl
who saddened him, being (in his poem)
from Kadango. At his navel-name
greeting, she floated to the next customer.

Lupenga's villagers were dismayed.
In their rain dance, the lightning cock struck
Beauty, charring her waist beads. "I'll
find out", said the chief, solemn and grieved.

"Up at Katoro you see the red sky"
wrote exiled Scopas, dreaming
of his beloved Juba Town, its ashes
that stood like anthills under napalm.

Late in the night of our first safari
to tickle the censors of that Banda-stan,
my own was tabled: the chief's daughter
dancing to "The Seekers" outside her hut.

Briefs

In the Village

In the village
a deep debate:

The chief's daughter has a transistor;
she is dancing to the *Seekers*
gaily outside her hut.

But the tape-recorder man
on his codification project wants
"Your own music", he demands,
"Marimba! Bangwe!"

The chief is bemused
by this pressure from Europe
not to attend to Europe.

Is he "himself"
with the radio on or off?

Moments Musicals

On a mudbank the reed huts
flood when the river is in flood.
We stop by the well and enquire. Bangwe?
A man is sent for. No good.
The instrument has gone for repair.

But money? He produces the bangwe,
a contraption of wood and wires
and bottle caps tied to a biscuit tin.
And look! He has changed his costume,
English rags to African tatters.

Squatting he chirrups and strums.
I smile. The fishermen twist with laughter.
He tells me he has finished. Blind
To his blindness, I toss a florin.
Too much, says my companion.

Noble savage: noblesse oblige.

12

Supermarket

Oh delicate are the white
arms and delicatessen shoulders
of the white wives leaning (oh
delectable their cool breasts)
forward, row of white wrists
arched in demand,
                   and so
polite the black salesmen, such
un-negritudinal corncob smiles,
tendering
from pools of blood
delicious breast, liver, steak, chops, shoulders.

Indeed Of Course We Must All Respect

our customs,
said the businessman
leaning on the wing of his Mercedes,

our folklore,
said the lecturer
working another proverb into his novel,

our morals,
said the husband
burning the pamphlets and the mini-skirt,

our justice,
said the chief Chief
detaining his opponents without trial,

while the ninety-six per cent (all
indeed of course respect the four)
are elbowed to the edge of their own world.

When Livingstone Stared at the Lakeshore

When Livingstone stared at the lakeshore,
purging his boyhood in dreams of cotton,
did bouncing, honey-limbed girls
toss him a beachball?

When the presbyters broached their Galilee
with all hands psalming the Old Hundredth,
did they signal *The Moor's Head*
for whiskies and soda?

Visionaries, name-givers, lavish exiles,
reject their fantasies, but fear
that ulcered woman washing pots,
those blank, huge-bouldered mountains.

Dhow Crossing

*'Photographers should not miss Leopard Bay, where
colourful dhows land regularly'*

(Malawi Holiday Guide).

The lake pitches in its void.
Invisible, the headlands
anchor a starless night.
A light winks from nowhere.
Watch. Faintly, the dawn glimmer
separates to a skyline.
The marked island bulges.

14

In morning, nondescript,
a washed-up coconut husk
bleaching on the horizon.
Watch. Slowly, as perfect shadows
shorten to the beach-huts,
it blanches, moon-struck.
But what? What-can-on-earth it's

birdshit! An island
ghastly with birdshit,
boulder and grass and brachystegia
shitlicked to a thin
icecap! Watch. Vaguely, heat
drains the bayscape
to sepia, but the island

glows like a presence, like
bones in flashlight
littering caves hyenas
have abandoned, or that eggshell
skull your fingers tip-touch
under the white shampoo
when your eyes avoid the mirror.

Memo: a colourful
subject for photography.
Watch. Ghostly, from such
absence, such a hole
in daylight (now sickening
to the yellow-green fluorescence
of fever trees), might not

dhows advance at dusk
rippleless on the chrome lake,

spectre slavers bonded
to enslaved ancestors?
All starless night the island
signals slave. I keep
expecting birdshit on my scalp.

At a Tangent

For these roadside markets we always
pull in. The sugar cane, maize cobs, sweet
potatoes, a brown paper twist of groundnuts,
cost nothing. But it isn't the money.

It's the living shadow, the neat pyramids
of colour, the peacock women, the courtesies
of purchase. As they tuck our small change
under their mats, our dust cloud settles.

Once, exhausted by the dirt road's
corrugations, we parked in a mango tree's
black disc. From the tall grass came
a woman, hoe on her forehead,

child on her back. She crossed
the road like a minefield, and into
the grass opposite, pursuing her
own journey at a tangent. Or we were.

For Captain Stedman

"I now must make an apology for my style, which is turn'd by G-d! so very insipid, that I myself am tired with it. D-mn spelling. d-mn writing, and d-mn everything overdone."

1

By G-d! Johnny, near pistoll'd
in your cradle, that pigeon's
crop you stuck up nanny's bum,
Jacobite schoolblows, raped
by your uncle's maid, and Mrs Mallet
tendering her carcass to an ensign,
lampoons and duels and haylofts,
punch and plackets, it makes
devilish fine reading!

and Joanna: not surprising
a mulatto slave girl be thrust
in somewhere, eh Johnny?
That's a ripe sketch you shape
of her, a ripe joke this nigger-
wench costlier than your fortune!
But wife? Two thousand florins?
A son? By G-d! Captain, that's
devilish unChristian!

2

Therefore at L'Esperance,
the colony at war,
you built your house
of grass and wattle,
a room for your girl,

17

a room for painting,
a kitchen, henhouse,
palisades, a bridge,

Captain and artist,
wounded in the campaign,
you carved a pool
downstream under
the bamboo lances,
whose amber
drenched her body
sheerest gold.

Soldier and lover,
the revolt subdued,
you limped nightly
barefoot through
the mangrove's
gothic doorways
to the Dutchman's plantation
and her side.

A grass and wattle
studio at L'Esperance;
if only there were
diamonds, you prayed
searching upstream;
if only fighting
rebel blacks sufficed
to buy her freedom.

3

Stedman, your Smollett-dabbed journal brags
loud of yourself, viz., I told the bugger
he ought to know a dog's turd from another
after getting so many, viz., I pass my time
making baskets for the girl I love, viz., d-mn
Order, d-mn Matter-of-fact, d-mn Everything!
and Captain you do, with five challenges
one month, no slight, no oversight, no lost
button or bruised bum too trivial to curse
and bring to cutlasses, yet such chivalrous
brawls, only with Captains! Johnny, you bore
a code in your fevers, far beyond Paramaribo
up brimming blackwater rivers where forests
choke in their creeper-hammocks, and Negroes
racked and handlopped, splintered on wheels,
hamstrung, scalded in sugar-vats, skewered
blistering by furnaces, and girls' breasts
mistress-whipped to blood for their masters'
fondling – Captain, your pen nib splutters Oh
Fie! for every gouge, brand, manacle, every
throat self-slit and earth eating, the horror
of nightly nightmares and Joanna's auction!

So what in the name of sketching are these
arabesques, these slender Egypto triangles
strutting the skylines of your history, viz.,
your *Narrative of a Five Year's Expedition
Against the Revolted Negroes of Surinam*?
Or these all-but-nudes? such poised despair,
such healthy breasts and thighs! are they
slaves, these buxom Maori-haired Italians?
Or Joanna, your dear dead girl, whose wife-
maddening monument to five years' loving

on the Wild Coast your book is, how can
poison lie in ambush for this lilting virgin,
a straw hat in her hand, this barefoot
gipsy with the tight curls, her dark breast
proffered to a curving, friendly world
of formal palms and odorous orange groves?
Stedman, your gentle melancholy Art
Distills the loyal chaos of your heart,
Weeps o'er the victims of a barb'rous Age,
But distances to Elegance, Outrage;
You could not murder Style to match their Life;
You saw not Slaves but Men and a dear Wife.

Lusaka Blues

1

    After the salad afternoon
parties on the sloping lawn,
My Lady's hands and the Police
ensemble um-pah-pah in glove,
    After the dawn arrests, the sad
lucky deaths, and oh My Lady's
party for the Commissioners,
His Excellency's Last Post,
    After the limp flag has taken
Empire's last sundowner, and so
on etc., look out man, pull
off the road, here comes

the Party! In fifty-four
limousines: each car contains
one member, each member
has a driver, each driver hugs

an escort of five howling
sirencycles. Desolate the tarred road
to that settlement of Indian shops
the Party calls a city.

2

Late afternoon we work in our separate gardens,
waving to each other from under lines of washing.
A lorry tours the estate collecting labourers.
The Party sirens are wailing on the airport road.
People will soon move into the redbrick flats
opposite the planned supermarket and petrol station.
There are swallows gathering on the telephone wires.
They look like heavy chords on a romantic score,
but whatever was once here has already departed.

Ministering

She has watched him rise and now he falls.
The radio denounces him. He returns
un-chauffeured, Benz-less, trudging the path
from the cotton depot where the lorry dropped him:
his paunch is heavy, his suit sweat-stained, he smells.

The children swagger in his wake. He mutters
at the anthills. It was tribalism, conspiracy,
his typists whoring. There was nothing else,
no reason. He was no different. The President
would learn things when he got his letter.

The path snakes through the village. What he didn't
see on the ministerial visit, in his soft world
of secretaries, his bitterness sees now.

The place is full of beggars, primitive, the thatch
rotting, reeds uncut, thistles in the cotton gardens.

She watched him rise. Now he returns. What accident
permitted it and what appetites propelled,
she knows. There is nothing to come back to.
The girls have gone, the young men have gone.
At the black door of her hut where burning cowdung

stuns the mosquitoes, she awaits her son.

After the Revolution

1

Before the coup, this ice-cool water sprang
where the summit boulders punched the cloudbase, and it
fell, a smoking slipstream, swallowed
by ravines, issuing under the tree ferns
down slopes of brachystegia
to the cool shade-grevilleas and carpets
of lush tea, and this
pool poised on a ledge above
the shimmering dusty town. Before the coup
the occupying troops eased
guns from their shoulders, dangling
bare feet in the water. Today along the bush tracks
it is the liberators who are being ambushed.
From the deserted pool we watch
the cortege leave the barracks. The fusillade
echoes round the mountainside, dying
at the boulders where the ice-cold water springs.

2

Hairy Dionysio, whose
missing eye-tooth isn't
mentioned by Euripedes,

malarial Dionysio, who
snared us with wine,
with pigeons for *petisco*,

kid-cutlets, giant
prawns, guinea-
fowl with coconut,

and brandy in
the lamp-lit store
he will not abandon

to the *Forças Populares*
throwing stones
at his paw-paws;

randy Dionysio, whose
brown, much-beaten
mistress bears

him annually
a child,
is perennial.

Across the road,
liberator Pentheus
is murdered;

there are new guerrillas

23

filing through
the tall grass.

Refugee

1

Old warm boulders in the sunlight,
terracing the garden where the jacaranda
burns above a crumbling path of bricks.
She is young. There is a panic
of monkeys in the bamboo. Dry spears
tumble and are brushed off her hair.
She is young. After the violence,
the floorboards wet with bloodstains,
she blossoms here, climbing. The veranda
draws her upwards with its scented violets:
I greet her with a glass of coconut milk.

2

The bombers strike, and shapes
in the photograph scatter, already dying:
the flames cling like water.
When the napalm
has eaten through their lives, only
bulldozers can assuage our horror:
the red trench swallows the charred corpses.

Bombers and grass huts,
and people in charity clothing queuing
for flour. It keeps raining
and is called revenge
for the tourists ambushed, the baby

hacked in bed, the burning
mission with its women raped and bludgeoned.

None of the guilty are killed:
the avaricious, the psychopathic,
the leaders, power-gluttonous.
But guilt, like human
flesh, clings. We eat, drink.
vote and read, and cannot honour
the graves or name a single murdered child.

3

Secure in giving orders, when the gunmen
turned to face him he could not believe it:
these were his instruments, and he above
contention in his palace of corridors.
They too were nervous. His confidence
swelling to an order, they opened fire.

Drumming! The ebony, peacock crowds!
Largesse on the radio, the detainees
released. With luck, two season's
respite while authority remembers
the corpse in the corridor. Two whole rains
before IT grows secure in giving orders.

4

Old colonial, burdened words
for this well-weathered house
and our pleasure in its charred

brickwork, its stone floors
glassy with age. Sunwashed
walls need no disguise

25

of creepers in the terraced
garden, whose mango and bamboo
and flame-cupped tulip trees

contain the broader view
of green plain, greener lake
and towering, ice-bound plateau.

Colonial: we enlightened migrants,
visiting the battlefield,
knowing what demands

passed downhill from this old
house, dropping on the bare
heads of headmen and elders

for taxes and labour,
we mendicants, treading
the minefield, know

our legacy as nothing
so well built. Timelessly, bricks
burn. There is shooting

on the hillside. Our book
grows slowly to the steady
swift chiselling of the clock.

5
Revisiting that house of terror
he found his anger burned away:
the blood-splashed floorboards were an error
which bloody dreams could not repay.

Now bombers shower the clustered tents
with napalm labelled retribution,
he honours all the innocents
for whom there can be no solution,

and boards his plane and flies in fear
to where the weaponry comes from:
the war will last another year,
but he is safe, and rich, and home.

The Safari Business

In old Zanzibar in the 1870s
the rising men were already in business,
Kiongwe, Chuma, Bombay, Wellington,
cashing in on a Victorian racket.

As the great explorer's steamship anchored
they were there, jostling in the lighters:
"What lake you want to visit, bwana?
We show you, isn't it? No problem!"

The 2 vol. quartos rolled from the press
How I discovered Lake Bangweolo,
and these guides, guards, nurses, catamites,
were rascally bearers and incompetent cooks.

It was ever so. The world's writ's
entangled with the power to inscribe
(Afterwards, when they'd discovered a little,
the safari business became *Whites Only*).

Bar Domino

Bar Domino was the border;
the café tables addressed
another country halfway across the road.

Beyond the chickenwire and dust
of the backyard and the sideyard
were frontier posts,

rubber stamps and guards
and guns,
uniformly bored.

This left Bar Domino
nowhere
between the valley and the mountain,

and everywhere:
we came for what was banned
behind our barriers,

valley subjects for the tainted
air of Independence,
the hill descenders

for decadence,
and we, separately expatriate,
for freedom from our choices

in wine and heat
and talk and sex and prawns
while Macielle, like a deity,

dispensed.
All this, being years ago,
has its appropriate cadence:

the countries, grown bolder
in disagreeing to agree,
Bar Domino has been claimed and closed.

Some of us have a memory
of tubular chairs and beer mats,
the bottle-coloured mango tree,

leaves and dust
arguing in whirlwinds,
and after dusk

a sluggish fan
churning the fug, as metaphor
for all-man's-land,

vivid beyond the frontiers,
different from all we have
and are,

the violable origins of love.

Sinking

after level hours through
thick folds of darkness,
jolting on the tarmac,
the spirit flares streaming
yellow tongues towards the plane,

stepping into the cloth-warm
saltodorous night air
of a small swamp with a gate,
the cicadas shrill and clouds
buzz-buzzing every bulb
on the white-trunked avenue
of skeletal flamboyants,
hunched low in the musty
fan-shuddered terminal bar,

I am back where imagination
sank its first wells.

Imprint

A literary country: we drank the local *Star*
in *The Heart of the Matter*'s Bedford Hotel,
where the whores had taken over and owner
Freddie was non-committal about Greene:

we paced the abandoned toy railway
from Fig Tree up to Hill Station, pausing
at Wilberforce, where Scobie agonised
in those swift, laterite-coloured dusks:

this crossed Crouchback, Waugh's alter-ego,
descending with that death-dealing bottle
smuggled to Apthorpe in the officers' hospital,
where we bivouacked for fifteen months.

Then there was *Hamlet*, performed in 1607
by the crew of the *Dragon*, in the silted estuary:
this consoled me, gazing down from my veranda,
though the art/nature link was never so tenuous.

Gentler than Growth

Gentler than growth, Sahara
dust settles on the mango
leaves, and ruffian hotel
taxis, blaring in their
dustclouds, trail laterite
grit, drycoating eyes, daubing
brick-red this pot-holed
street of huts and lean-tos,
sulphurous pawpaws, rusting cane,
a red pepper settlement
of gardener, porter, sweeper,
waiter, bellboy and bargirl,
dancer and curio-man,
season ticket holders
on an endless middle passage.
As places go, this is a place
to turn back from, despite
coconut flags unfurling
bronze to rasp the corrugations
of the iron-bound chapel,
its summoning harmonium
querulous as mosquitoes as
my taxi barks rescue.

Briefly in the rear mirror
cloud and ash are radiant;
the travellers walk through fire
to their twilight Lord.

Correspondence

"Friend, we got here last November:
I'm writing (sorry to take so long)
slung across our veranda
in a hammock. You were wrong
about the climate. We're a thousand feet
above it, on a clifftop facing the sea.
The house (hardly a shanty) is fine
except for the ants and a stray cat.
It's pleasant as Alice serves coffee
to stare at the hulks in the estuary:
the castaway, his dusky concubine.

Man Friday too! in the squatting
shape of a schoolboy in the cupboard
downstairs. Rather fitting
really, since we can't afford
the tools it's meant for, so we store
him as lawnmower, spade and sickle.
He's used to it up-country
mixing his lessons with agriculture.
It's good as I down a six o'clock
beer to enquire about his kinsfolk:
the kindly proprietor, the peasantry.

Today, there's two! Musa's note
'Sounds or syllables can't carry
your kindness to my schoolmate'
was entertaining – and why worry
when new boy knows his stuff? He trapped
the watchman shitting in the drains.
He found out who at 3.00 a.m. coughed
filth under our bedroom – and it stopped!

It works at breakfast to confront
Pompey with yesterday's complaints:
The promising D.C., his handpicked staff.

P.S. April. Bribed to efficiency,
the police are quite certain. Musa,
says Pompey, has taken money.
We check, are short, he is dismissed.
This year, we relax. After our deportation,
Pompey will laugh, sharing the beer
With soldier ants and the traitor
Tomcat, staring in hammocked isolation
At shanties a thousand feet inferior,
And nobody will move up downstairs:
the one-party state, the cool dictator."

Language as a Second Language

Sierra Leone has all right to be proud
    the chief object is as we conceive it
Of her lot to offer the world in respect
    to demonstrate and inspire to this class
        Ha! Watch out. Enemy about you.
Of the ability of her sons and daughters
    though by no means lacking in curiosity
Who are given opportunity and co-operation
    or destitute of sensibility to literature
To display their talents and offer great
    new avenues of thought through the medium
        Any man can be a fool
And yet greater things to the world if
    of critical analysis and synthesis
And only if there is stability and self-help

33

what we confidently anticipate is that
Status quo and forgetting of old scores
    through this class whose benefit we have
        Your best Friend is your secret Enemy
Let those who have talent be encouraged
    in view and which we inadvertently believe
For many have not crossed the Rubicon
    there will be a moral and intellectual
But allow their talents to be dormant
    improvement that many hours which might
        Nor God no save We
Creative men and women of Sierrra Leone
    otherwise be wasted in folly and vice
Please give wings to your imagination
    will be employed in pursuits which while
And produced great things yet undreamed of
    they afford the most lasting pleasures
        Money don, Baby leh
For the admiration of the developed world
    are not only harmless but purifying
And the cultural pride of Sierra Leone
    and edifying for the liberation of Africa
        No matter how you sabi Book you noh go Pass

A Girl's Best Friend

Thigh-deep, sluicing the sulphurous mud,
he palmed it to his mouth, a gin-pink
rhomboid lozenge, worth
a year's wages – He offered it for a day's.

Immortal diamond. The atomic sun
in minature. At forked lightning, men said,
they zigzagged underground. Small wonder
the state was undermined in the ultimate

national lottery. Not a school, hospital,
market or highway was safe from these
fundamentalists, these delvers for the base
as all collaped. Diamonds, till death

us depart. There was something Homeric
about such frenzy, viz., the 40-man dugouts
crossing at sunset, paddled with shovels,
for another night's raid on the sinking fund.

Province of Freedom

The Botanical Gardens (former
War Department Property Keep
Out, former bush) are

bush again, lianas wrapping
gun mounts and dog-Latin
tags, a python's grip

on ironwood and the cannon-
ball tree threatening the track
I carried Martin down

across the once-bridged brook
and up to Heddle's ruined Farm.
A viewpoint: easy to overlook

from here the plunging slum
of Freetown, or under this
shade trade where anthuriums

run wild now to erase
those shadow freemen, their
darkness like a bruise,

their dancing solitaire,
ankles shackled
to their record player.

Heddle's dreams of pastoral
composed this second garden;
even now the sun angles

lightly through light-green
decks of guava, drenched
with bright flamboyant

down to this wooden bench
and Martin sleeping
in my arms. Branches

light with foliage keep
boughs heavy with flowers
raised, and I wrap

Martin tight, and stare
aloft through verdant arches;
it is peaceful here.

A viewpoint: but the watchers
(are there eyes behind
those shades?) approach:

they are not impassioned,
they are not impressed,
this is no-man's-land:

I fold my brown son closer to my breast.

Distances

Someone said you could buy chicken manure
in the hills, above Charlotte and Waterloo,
so I drove with Jalloh, sackcloth and a spade,
bumping the tarmac through the rain forest

where the orchids I wanted to grow grew
wild and chimpanzees, strap-
hanging above us, hooted insults
at my Imp. Climbing, we surfaced

at a twilit clearing. As promised, it was dirt
cheap. My spade was redundant as Mamadu
took charge. I asked Jalloh, "How'd you
fancy living up here?" "It far," he muttered.

Mamadu, shovelling shit, straightened.
"Far?" he exclaimed. "From WHERE?"
That raw pastoral has remained with me.
A cock crowed. The sun dropped on the instant.

Scribble

So, the Swedes the blonde gods have abdicated,
the push-button saw-mill is abandoned.

In its twilight. mildew summons
vox humana of mosquitoes.

Outside in the day glare the far bank
fades to sepia, its fringe of palms dancing.

They were planning ho! ho! ho! these tall efficient
vikings with their bearded earnestness

that anthill and baobab, the river drifting with its
                                    islands, the flapping herds
trumpeting down the mushroom huts and hut-high millet

be sawn, sanded, cooled, refined
to a white rectangle of paper like this one.

They are not the first
whose blank eden sprung a serpent.

Sugar men, copra men, tea, sisal, tobacco men
have all before loaded their ships and departed.

There are ruined engines of antiquarian value
corroding on all the river estates.

But nothing so fine as the saw-mill
shining blonde at the farm's edge, where a woman

hunchbacked with child is hoeing poverty,
still waiting for a god prepared to scribble.

From Robert Moffat's Journal, 1854

"4th June, Sabbath, the afternoon
cloudy and cold. Under the *mosetla* tree
I once addressed Senthuhe and his men.
The whole town has been burned off
by the Boers. No piles of stones,
broken pillars, tessellated pavements,
nor the shadow of a street, nor anything,
remain to tell 1000s once lived here.
Charred stumps peep here and there
through the ground, with two or three
skulls shot cruelly by the Boers,
and cats too, said one, watching my kittens.

Sebobi, hearing of wagons, came down
from the summit and his people emerged.
After coffee, I assembled them and preached.
I talked with him on the importance
of attending to divine things but, alas,
he is very far from the kingdom of God.

All will be ordered by Him who knows
our hairs' number and sees the sparrow fall
(there are no sparrows here. I had thought
them everywhere. Like flies and crows)."

Cotton, Rubber, Tobacco etc.

"So now you are going to have your coffee?"
says the interpreter approvingly,
and the villagers gather in a noisy circle to study
the white man drinking his coffee.

They have all grown coffee for the white man
and can tell me about every stage
of the culture and preparation – except for the drinking
which is hilarious to watch.

Who knows? Next I might change my underpants,
blow up a condom, burn
a cigar, or do something else they have worked
lives for and never earn.

Chimwalira

The truth is he was born at Chimwalira
not Bethlehem. For Immanuel the conception
was a good one. But it was hard in a place
without writing to show prophecies fulfilled.
She gave birth on a reed mat in a mud house,
but so did every woman. How much grander
a stable signifying property in the foreground.
So when the Magi appalled by the Nile's
green wilderness turned back worshipping
a Jewish boy in a safe colony, they missed
their star's conjunction with Crux Australis
and God lay forgotten in Africa.
                        Chimwalira,
"where someone died". He grew up ordinarily,

neither Tarzan nor Shaka, eating millet
and wild mice. After his circumcision
there were songs about his dullness with women.
He became a blacksmith and a doctor skilled
in exorcism, and people saw he was touched.
But there was nothing startling to the elders
in his proverbs. He died old at thirty-three,
a normal life span.

       (It was the Reverend Duff McDuff
screamed the Python priest was the Black Christ
as they led him to his steamer in their straightjacket.)

Words for Heroes' Day, perhaps

Being in the Welsh style uninclined to give politicians
credit for the brilliant acts their speeches enjoin us
to applaud on their tightrope strung between banks,

nor finding congenial the climate of cenotaphs,
rituals of death as though death were sacrifice
and sacrifice legitimised those hierarchies of stamping,

not being, in short, in any sense *imbongi* or praise poet,
whether sweeping thorns from the ruler's path or brandishing
a symbolic knobkerrie as spokesman for the people,

I am in the English manner a little at a loss to find
words for this anniversary when visiting after Empire
I am asked to pay tribute to those who died for Freedom.

That some were heroes is quite certain though not
necessarily the men on the platform (nor necessarily men).
Even the dead are ambiguous. Remembering them I think

most of those innocents cremated in their hundreds
as fire rained on the camps where they were queuing for flour.
Calling them heroes makes their slaughter seem called for

though their ghosts cry out for an eternal flame of anger.
Even among the warriors there were, as we too well understood,
the psychopathic who will never settle to justice.

But though irony has no heroes there is a poetry of facts.
There were others (not necessarily the men on the platform)
who are already legend and their legend a gracious one,

speaking of pastoral, the column filing through the tall
grass to a clearing with huts in the hut-high millet
and a shining welcome from the old who remembered the Rising,

speeches, courtesies observed with prayers to the ancestors,
songs and dancing, the girls crazy with admiration,
the meal from a shared pot when even a bean was divided,

then at moonrise moving onwards to the dawn's target,
and though doubting whether half of this happened or whether
half of that half matters in the unchanged city,

I honour them for the metaphors they died for. That
they made strutting ridiculous, if only momentarily,
is sufficient for our homage. May their ghosts

snatch at these anklets rattling today for our applause.

The Accord

The ambassador's wife greets with a kiss
Xavier, pot-bellied, hair growing out of his ears.

In his slim heyday he founded a dozen newspapers
and lost interest in them. The secret police

of six dictatorships had him on their files
though his insignificance kept him out of their jails.

Now he's a raconteur with a whisky in his hand,
a man to be courted, the right ear of the president.

He has been comrade to an alphabet of revolutionaries,
Amilcar, a true Marxist despite the controversies,

David who turned to the bottle when his poetry dried up,
Eduardo, Herbert, Marcelino, Philipe,

and Samora the victor whom, after fourteen years
of excoriating defectors, he advised to make peace

(though Nelson and Walter were still on Robben Island).
Xavier is writing a book about necessity and the dialectic

and his own career in cellars and public libraries,
those endless trains, third class, across central Europe,

and an article explaining about Dar es Salaam
based on Lazaro's letters and a diary kept at the time,

and a pamphlet analysing why the nation is in crisis.
The ambassador's wife is glassy-eyed listening to this.

43

The whisky bottle's hourglass has too long to run.
"How can you know," she says, "the right people will win?"

Xavier is disconcerted. He is not used to disagreement.
He was hardly aware there was a woman present.

"How do you stop it ending in a lot of nastiness?"
Is she a liberal? Or just stupid? A waste

of time explaining. He searches for Latin courtesy
just as she too is remembering necessity

and they smile like conspirators as she reaches
for the bottle, pours two fingers and signals the kitchen.

Theoretician-pragmatist, Xavier bows to the accord,
gets a peck at departure as his gallantry award.

Thief

The heat is on. We sleep
naked, starting at broken glass.

What will he feel the slippery
thief interrupted in the living room,

who has kept me hours by the smashed
door with this sharpened cutlass,

what will be his rage he grabbed
only the bassoon concerto K191?

Benighted under a toenail moon
the tin roof signs, contracting.

The fridge offs. In shocking quiet
a cockroach smacks the lampshade.

The nightjar whistles like someone
jumping sing-sing on a wire fence.

I am tuned for violence. I make
arpeggios with the cutlass. Images are

that head and hand through the jagged
frame and my striking bloodily.

Nightlong I appease witches.
With cockcrow the denials cease.

But what of him in his mud shack
in the *bairro* angry with Mozart?

Beauty, patronage, such order: shivering
he might well come back to kill.

Mozambique, Flying

Trees rise alone from the pools
of their own shadows and clouds
float above their shadows, the jet's
toy shadow moving through them
like a ghost.

They exist rock and thornscrub,
the sepia dustscape, trees
parched and nervous, and a huge sky
drained pale, the jet
a silver hornet;

but at cloudheight, with the one
road a winding scribble
I could brush off with my sleeve,
it is hard to remember
what one knows,
or to guess at bombed villages,
bodies unburied, festering
unburied. Untenanted, like clouds,
our scything shadow merges
with shadows.

The Base

Studiously, the villagers misled. For an hour
they kept us circling, until someone pointed
and I parked in a grass-walled compound.
Three huts. Flour bags. A thatched dormitory.

The woman rinsing uniforms in the corner
ignored us as Alice prepared Martin's bottle.
I was spreading the roadmap on our 127's
bonnet when a dozen armed guerrillas

sprang from ambush. "Oh, there you are", I said,
smiling at the circle of Kalashnikovs.
Long afterwards, Rafael told me it was
the baby proved us harmless. At the time,

this all seemed normal. The commandant
gave me a letter: *The bearer* (of such idiot
nonchalance) *is a friend and wherever
he goes we request he should be well-treated.*

Joanna

1

The hardest part, writing the account
A dozen years after in a another country,
The hardest memory was her utter
Separateness. She had lain in his arms
So soft, so pliable, he was the bridge
Straining above her, drowning
In her depths as she ebbed to the sea.
He was the leaky dam at L'Esperance.

Writing the account, her death made
Believable his lost age of gold.
But he knew it was never so. For
All the rich tapestry of poems
He wove round her, a fuck
Was a fuck. It left her untouched.

2

I was slave, not so? The hardest
Part was he touched me with hope.
Not in bed as he pounded me
With his soft pestle, but after
When sweettalk could get him no more
And he sang his poems. He built me
A pool at L'Esperance by the gold
Waterfall. I loved him, nearly.

But he's just a man. No money, like
My father. Soon he'd want younger
Girls to pound out his pride, and where
Would I hide in England? So I laughed.
When he married I smashed my mortar
And drank my poison. And felt sure.

Parts of Speech

Dictation was just that, the chief Chief
pronouncing in a land where everything
(hemlines, blood-doning) was political
except the politics. If his Daimler passed

the rule required a fullstop, later, a stop
plus applause. Neutrality was sentenced,
and I learned in friends the heroism
of question marks, the ramifications for wife

and child to the tenth cousin of dotting
the 'I's of the script. Worse, how
yearning for a grammar of nationhood
spawned timid modifiers. Or secret verbs.

The country braked, of course. The worst
mimicked, the best were banished or detained.
My deportation conferred spurious credit
on one whose asides were well insured.

The Ethiopian Woman

When ageing Moses took as his umpteenth wife
the Ethiopian woman,

Aaron and his own wife Miriam
howled the tabernacle down.

So God descended in a pillar of thunder:
Moses was a true prophet, his word

was HIS word, and when the holy tornado
dispersed, Miriam found herself a leper.

Even Moses (there's an insert here,
claiming he was the mildest of men) even

he balked at this crime against humanity.
Caught in his prevarications, God

modified the sentence. If a man
spat in his wife's face, she was banned

from the camp seven days and nights. So
a restored Miriam served a week's exile,

all this in the Sinai, while the chosen people
were pining for those wet cucumbers

and Egypt's staff-of-life garlic. No one
comes well out of this tale, not

Moses with his tented master bedroom, nor
those proto-Afrikaners with their mixed-marriages

cant, nor God, a petulant Hastings Banda,
with his paraphernalia of magic.

Only the Ethiopian, her silences
silenced, lives in cultured rebuke.

What Lion Spits Out

What lion spits out, Jack said, *must be tough*.
I was flattered. Afterwards, on the VC10
banking north-east over the brimming river,
I saw it in different light as wise counsel.

Once from a dugout on that swift, pewter
river, I watched the slim jet tilting north.
Banished, I stared down at the baobabs:
where snake suns himself must be comfortable.

A country of passive verbs. Deported
(my 48 hours sentence) or detained
(Felix was the first of our group to rot):
when hippo yawns, the pool dries up a little.

Taban was brusque, Okot pre-occupied
with harsher wrongs. It was re-resurrected
Ngugi who talked me through my pain
(active voices, *A Grain of Wheat*).

Immortal Diamond

(Jack Mapanje, detained 25 September 1987)

Outside the bar, night, bullfrogs promising rain,
the sky a dome of stars ripped
by the black edge of the mountain.

Bloated face, trunk like a baobab,
"We've got your lame friend,"
from the unmarked jeep

boasting special branch. Words hidden
a hemisphere off grudge
"Now you're on your own,"

and I can smell here the Carlsberg
on his breath. He leers
from the smuggled page.

Lame: alone: "we're
preparing a place for him."
This clown knows the power

Of pauses, the ecstasy of rhythm.
His threat is accurately
their dread. For Jack, our dear friend's poems

are out, unparoled, his meta-
phors dancing from lip
to lip and no heavyweight

knuckles ripping
pages
can stop

them. The crippled swagger
"We've got your friend,"
calms outrage

at that night, that frog-loud prison yard, leaned
on by the mountain, where Jack, joke, patch,
matchwood, hardens

like starlight, needing no crutch.

2

Room for Autumn

We knew from the start this was a room
to listen to Brahms in. Westering,
watching the stockade wall at sundown,
it was a room for autumn and we tiled
one wall in yellows and cello brown
with poachers in the reed thickets
where the piano leaps peremptorily
bringing the falling fourths to resolution;
a room for books and a log fire
and love-making on the gold chesterfield.

Politics in the basement where the Irish
navvy lived blows its dust of a century
upwards. Through stretched chords,
long-fingered tenths, a dry harmattan
whistles. Bunched chromatic runs
from the gas lamp rising cannot
wall it out. We are restless having
witnessed blood. There is a fountain
daily over the narrow water where
murder is a hymn in sixteen bars.

Crafted music: the stockade at night
is the colour of the owl that keeps us
watching. We knew from the start
there would be trouble composing
a room hollowed out by all we have
lived through. Counterpoint is one
of our words, tiles with their poetry
and the milk-white wall. And Brahms,
classicist with a dying fall. Autumn comes
even to the most unreconciled of believers.

Castaway, N.W.1

A charcoal mind is needed
for these grey perspectives,
not this brain coral
aching for lagoons,
on the horizon a schooner
pounded to driftwood.

Is this, after all,
the landscape I deserve,
a pulpit for irony?
The London sky
drapes like a cobweb
over towers and steeples.

Do they find us
or we our metaphors?
Here on Primrose Hill,
the leaves falling,
do I take colour
or recognise myself?

Anxiety of Influence

I was 17 when, blessed suddenly with gold,
I happened in the sixth form library
on Blunden's *Poems of Wilfred Owen*.
He had sat in this self-same dormitory,

engulfed in the same masturbatory
rebellions, the same teen-age passion

for Keats, the same hatred of *Birkenhead*
Institute for the Sons of Artisans.

What did I learn? That one of the names
on the school's War Memorial, poppied
annually to reproach us, had a voice.
That technique is subliminal, a device

of rhetoric, his half rhymes echoing
shell shock. That poetry doesn't flinch.
That it matters by calling poetry into
question. That he made pity heroic.

Lark

At greylight, lark is up there
while night hugs the kerbstones,
handful of bone and cartilage
blazing away like a transistor.

Has the fluttering creature crouched
hours in the lank verges,
lungs brimming with song?
At a glimmer, lark rises.

From the high dawn notes
shrill, precipitating
day. The motorway
hardens to light and noise.

Buddleia

From next door's patch the butterfly bush
is an indigo Niagara.

High above the purpling vine, it
thunders on our lake of michaelmas daisies,

and all hours of October daylight
painted ladies, tortoiseshells, cabbage whites, dashing red admirals

flock in flocks to its whirlpools.
At nightfall, when hawk moths mope and the swallows

have mutated to bats, they are
still there basking with the roaring in their ears, deaf

to the Minster's bells punching the night air.
It is an attitude to poetry and darkness.

Red Alert

You, the scientist on the coconut
island with a bunker and flotsam
of lubricious girls, cloning
yourself to rule the earth;

you, the double-agent hurtling
down the corridor while explosions
mount to a fireball, the silkiest
blonde undulating in your arms;

you, the man at the traffic lights

waiting for green, you are far
madder, you with the supermarket
trolley, you with the pension.

The View from the Stockade

1
From the stockade is a view of pastoral
lost, our fields and gardens
wasted by the enemy.

For years the city appalled us but
when the hordes came where
else was refuge?

From the stockade we watch thistles
swarm. We have our wives here
and water. We shall survive.

all but the heartsickness, our innocence
undone. Now there begin
ledgerbooks, usury.

2
"He's ca-ca-cantankerous," she stuttered.
It was her one English word
almost, and where in Yorkshire did she
find it, this Black woman
with her pig farmer, up
in the Dales? As she
woke at five, mucked out the sties,
she swore back in Acholi
with a ripeness his mind shut out.

"He's ca-ca-cantankerous," she stuttered
to the Race Relations men
in her distress. There was nothing
they could do but open a file.
Why had she followed him
home from the army? She had
nothing to go back to. What silks
did she expect? And he? What
had he hoped to harvest of his rutting?

3

An old man striding, brittle in an anorak,
weathered as his walking stick, his wife
in a duffle coat, hand on his arm, together
halt in Sampson Square, once Thursday market.
"Once Thursday Market", he exclaims. "Aha!"
she says, brightening.
     An old couple
discovering what they were looking for,
rhythms of pastoral in the traffic jams.

Per se

With my cheque from *Poetry Wales*
she bought a bikini. Was Art ever
more rewarded, keeping
a steady eye on Nature?

On a Painting by William Etty

Towards the end he painted
pheasants, plumed iridescent
cock and drab hen together
limp with apples and mirrored nuts
on an oak table.
            This was
long after London, his vast
canvasses of allegory, when
Truth and Chastity came to Fall
with breasts so veined, so rosebud-tipped
impropriEtty they joked.
                  The journeyman
homed to Yorkshire where the gentry
gunned pheasants. There is all
sadness in this shattered
wing, fuschias, purples, yellow
accusing iris.
            Towards
the end he painted miniatures,
girls' faces mapped
with autumn, and these
stiffening overdressed game birds,
fruits, fruits.

Spain

It is May Day in Madrid, the old men march.
They are from Kent and Yorkshire. They shake
fists, chanting "Viva! Viva!" From among
the geraniums, the señoritas wave.

It is the old men's day. What world
did their ancient battles once occur in?
Hill Four-Eight-One, panting to the crest,
the enemies' faces white and visible.

Now they return, talking of thyme
and rosemary, and fallen comrades,
and of one absent, whose ashes
reverently they scatter under the olives.

Ordinary and old, today they swagger.
From red-splashed verandas, the dark girls
smile. Who does not admire them?
Which of us will passion keep so young?

Tales of the Islands

(after Derek Walcott)

Manchester Fête

If you see the fête! It had Jamaican,
Barbadian, Grenadian, Trinidadian,
like they making they own federation in Englan',
an' one seta fellars from the li'l islands
like St Kitts an' them, where you cyan't run fast
or you go fall in the sea, an' all they just
calling theyself West Indian 'cause
what you ever hear 'bout St Eustacius?

But if you see the fête! O God, no rum!
no calypso! No steelban'! Is only
Guinness an' Rolling Stones! They play some
Sparrow tune 'bout English Society

an' take the record off 'cause it too crude.
Yes, man, is true! Those fellars too damn integrated.

Concert, Free Trade Hall.

Despers, we know that short for *Desperadoes*
Steelban', it come *Gay Desperadoes* when those
Yankees study how you could sell they cokes
an' they frighten for a badjohn name, but look
this *Trinidad Philharmonic Steel orchestra* –
where you pick up that Afro-college culture,
Black Power classics by Johann Sebastian X?
What arseness you go be selling next?

Eh but those pans! That bass could really kick!
It have one double-tenor like the noteself talking.
Despers, is good you show these Englishmens
what you could do with they big famous tunes,
but I proud, proud you beat them j'ouvert style,
rough, fas', loud, like Laventille.

The Latest Rod

It was Scorpion told me limbo dancers
was either Pepsi or Coke. He doubled
as fire-eater ("Don't ever breat' in",
he warned), and dancer on broken glass.

One Sunday practice he came up the trace
limping, his heel bandaged. "A bottle
cut it right here in my yard". Five Past,
who did striptease, laughed (she was blacker

63

than her twin who was born at midnight).
"On stage," he said. "dey does heap it up".
It gave Lord Keskidee, our calypsonian,
his road march. But he missed the joke

of me on bass, doubling as impresario
to the Augustans and late Romantics
(memo: Pepsi/Coke bottles measured the height
of the latest rod they had to limbo under).

Charcoal

There is a moment when the wood has caught
and the charcoal has done its tinkling
and glows lasciviously, when
the carafe of *Dão* or *Quinta da Bacalhoa*
simmers in our talk
of long delayed summers peering
down at long last down
our well between the terraced houses
north north north
on our tiles and towel of lawn,

there is a moment when the fumes of burning
lamb with origanum, bay leaves and onions,
drift across the rag of lawn
to the brick wall where I'm reading
Walcott or Sebastião da Gama
or Dafydd ap Gwilym slagging
January, purring over May
and his burning trysts
in the improbable holly bush,
at that moment all our summers merge

in a scent so quick I don't know
what I'm remembering but, before
reductive words, happiness
floods, stinging my eyelids,
and I walk to where you are turning
skewers and I hold
your waist while you press
my wrists with your elbows:
all summers with wine and charcoal
are dark with south and south is you.

For her Wedding She Wore her Breasts Bare

For her wedding she wore her breasts
bare with woven beadwork at her waist
and plaited beadwork in her hair.
The girls sang, begging her
never to leave them for the bridegroom's mat.
Her heart soared as they drew her to his hut.

In Leeds she wears a dufflecoat and headscarf.
Her straightened hair is shielded from the rain.
Her husband at the Poly studies husbandry.
He is proud his village wife is wearing jeans.
She pushes her packed trolley round Tesco's,
black, pregnant, angry, missing

cowdung smouldering in the soft dusk as
cattle praises echo from the kraals.
The woodsmoke curls from cooking fires.
The children demand stories
or a lick of the ladle. Darkness drops.
The men come home in blankets with their pipes.

Ruanda

The wine spreads on the tablecloth,
Bloodstains darken on the sand.
I do not want to look at these pictures
Which knock my heart and my hand
Spilling, as lives are spilt in that land.

It was country fat with leaves.
Beans and pawpaw jumped where you threw them.
Who could forget such serious smiles,
Such courtesies if once you knew them?
What gods have done this to them?

A freckled girl, her hair distracted,
Gestures to the milling refugees.
Somehow, it seems, she is responsible
For their flour and water. How can this be?
Has all this been done to flatter me?

At the heart of where we come from
Is the mark of what we are.
My hand scrubs at the wine stain,
My eyes turn from the horror
(Far downstream, the corpses drift ashore).

War Poem

The hundred hours of Desert Storm
I was watching my lawn
    for bulbs springing
(the rest is for those who were there).

There may be a time for requiem
or selfless eulogy in Arabic
    or possibly English,
but which of us will write them?

Our passionate craft (to cut
the diamond metaphor,
    ridicule all
courtiers, burnish the other

in ourselves) dwindled
when it broke
    on our screens,
shaming first person singulars.

These poems of yours,
sniffing fastidiously
    at soldiers'
argot, raping attention

with the very horrors they deplore,
they preen, they comply
    with violence:
you were none of you in any danger.

The seven days of Port Stanley
I was studying
a village in Africa
(the rest is for those who were there).

Obituaries: Up 'an Under

21 January, aged 43, Countess 'Titi' Wachtmeister
   6 February, aged 83, William Younger GC
Model and sometime companion to Peter Sellers
   Hero of the Louisa Colliery disaster when 19 men
Along with King Gustav and ex-Beatle George Harrison
   Died in the blast or from snorting firedamp
(Condemned as 'vulgar' by the Crown Estates office
   He was at the coal face with two fellow deputies
When he tried to re-name his nightclub 'Titi's'
   And before midnight explosions wracked the seam).

Titi, with the looks of a blonde Jean Shrimpton
   But Younger knew all the shafts and roadways
A successful cover girl when she burst on London
   And ignored danger, clambering to the scene through
Parties and diplomatic modelling and society balls
   Derailed tubs and galleries choked with dust
Where Ben Ekland, Brit's brother, introduced Titi
   His canary dead, his lamp glowing barely a foot,
To Sellers, still married to Lord Mancroft's daughter
   And wrestled with his colleagues for almost two hours
Igniting a passion, despite their age difference,
   To move the injured and dying to a safer drift
But it ended in a wrangle over a Cartier watch
   Enabling five miners to be stretchered to the surface
Along with Titi's jewels and a favourite stuffed dog.

Gossip predicted marriage to King Gustav, but Titi
   Awarded the George Cross for gallantry
Wed Enrico Monfrini, a Geneva-based corporate lawyer
   Younger, modest and self-depreciating
The wedding attracted 150 jet setters

After almost half a century in the pits,
Including Gunter Sachs and Dai Llewellyn
   A grieving widower with two proud daughters
But a plumper Titi emerged from her separation
   Embodying the staunchness of the mining community
With a line of high-priced T shirts called 'T-T's Ts'
   (He bore his failing predicate with courage).
                    (adapted from *The Times*, 10 February, 1993)

Tongues

The Helen of my verse has four tongues:
last, convent English, a dialect of rank
and baffling insinuations. My bald
syntax, laced with irony, freezes.

We met in chiNyanja, the dictator's
brogue, dangerous for lovers, when a kiss
could land you in Kanjedza. The sounds
of silence, whispered behind closed doors.

Her schooling was Portuguese. It made her,
ran the myth, civilised. It turned her,
burgeoned the fact, rebellious. A lingo
to stand no nonsense, not least from husbands.

But hear her in chiSena, her mother's
creole, knees spread, elbows akimbo,
her lips curled in fertile obscenities,
earthed, lacking only a pipe!

Blueprint
(for Angus Calder)

I was born in 1940, the night of the fall of France,
My mother hated Churchill but my father wore the pants.
From my nappies I was short-changed on phlegm and nonchalance
   But Nightingales sang, etc.

My memory's a blank slate till 1943.
By then, the tale was shatterproof, chalking out mystery,
But something in those blank days has inked its tread on me
   We'll meet again, etc.

Dunkirk, the Blitz, the Spitfire few, my father had it pat,
Good and evil, black and white, Hamburg's tit-for-tat
(My mother would have hailed in blood a women's coup d'etat)
   Run, rabbit, run, etc.

What happened between them when fire fell from the sky
I don't know, I'll never know, swaddled in my
Premature cotton drawer cot, with *Li-*
   lacs in the spring again, etc.

Afterwards, my neckhair bristling at sirens, the sliver
-silver fuselage between cloud puffballs for once and ever
"That's Jerry" and balloons ears, afterwards or never
   There'll be bluebirds over, etc.

Till the pathescope begins with Dave Waddell's Messerschmidt
(He called it an altimeter, he'd got it from an Austin)
Smuggled along the back row of "Yield not to temptation",
   Don't sit under the apple tree, etc.

And Joyce Hopkinson spiking her hand on the ARP barbed wire,
How we laughed at her shrieking, tugging at her knickers
Until crimson on her left elbow satisfied our anger,
    You'd be so nice to come home to, etc.

And with the child's sure instinct of dark things suppressed
(Was he truly erect in the Blitzkrieg's caress?
Did she openly exult with Armageddon at her breast?)
    Who do you think you are kidding? etc.

How could I live with such perfections of bereavement,
The righteous logic of Germany's bedevilment?
I longed for ambivalence as a honed achievement
    Lili Marlene, etc

Till a film from "lands beyond the seas" kindled my qualms
With its tale of swamps and idolatry. Disbelief could blossom
With its feet in mangrove, its crown among the palms
    I've got a luverly bunch, etc.

I praised the cafe tables of a dust yard between frontiers,
The plank-and-oil-drum pontoons crossing rivers in the delta
The city on the sandbank with its conspiratorial poets
    Knock on wood, etc.

Till there came another war. It is waged by brutalised
Children. Some are just 12. They have mutilated
Or been forced to eat their parents. And they accumulate.
    If the sun should tumble from the sky, etc.

71

The Art

My hunt's for the found poem,
the one that finds me, and not
in a book or newspaper, its words
already bolted into place, but

out there in what really occurs
to us or me or them, so instantly
a birth happens like a new bud
on the moonflower, or over time

a pattern flickers like candleflies,
and in creating just what took place
so even the Fiat's number plate
is unchanged, my job's to find

a style so transparent you don't
hear any voice of mine shouting
Look at Me, just the depths gleaming
without a ripple to refract the art.

Self-Praises

(for my African age-mates)

I climbed the old elm tree and read *William* books in the
    rook's nest,
My knee stuck in the pulpit rail: for once the congregation
    laughed,
The missionary told of the poison ordeal: I was spellbound
    in the cub hut,
I won the match by slicing a six off the back of the bat over
    backward point,

I cycled a hundred miles precisely to Nettlebed and back to
     town,
I planted crotons, a whole hedge in thirty-two varieties,
I scored Sparrow's *Melda* for the steelbands' *Panorama,*
I made love to the circuit-minister's wife in a dark corner of
     the canefield,
I decamped from the island under an arch of leaping dolphins,
Baboons jumped on my steaming bonnet as I stalled on the
     escarpment,
I crossed the longest bridge at dusk, reading of another
     country,
I found her on a sand dune where a coconut palm strained at
     its bole,
She to whom all metaphors return was outlined with
     chevrons,
She stretched like a tigress, adorned with her stripes,
I watched the Beetle spinning downstream, swept from the
     flooded causeway,
My dugout parted the hyacinths in search of the hidden
     history,
When the armed guerrillas ambushed us, I said *Oh, there you
     are,*
From four jobs I resigned,
From the fifth the President deported me, without rhyme or
     explanation,
I helped at my son's birth: he came out looking dumbfounded,
My proudest expedient, bribing our baby on to the plane!
The professor rang at midnight: my poem was a masterpiece,
I designed and built a kitchen to a millimetre's calculation,
I knuckled down to fifteen years of mortgages and pension,
I campaigned for my dear friend to step forth like Lazarus,
My vine, in Viking territory, was a miracle of survival,
My garden exploded in poppies and cornflowers: autumn
     blazed in nasturtiums,

He wrote marvellously of his resurrection: it was I gave the
    writing space,
They shook hands, enemies to the vein,
They shook hands and reminisced across my conference
    table,
(The student wrote: *thank you, who else could we have got
    drunk with?),*
As a scholar, I set the paradigm: as a poet I found my niche,
Let these praises float from my window, setting fires where
    they will.

The Web

Our marriage spirals from the page (name
me a poet who bowed to his muse's
grandmother – or cousins, not to mention
sisters who, in the custom of her people,

could have been my wives too) which
is where our lovers' leap defies gravity,
for when Drennon, the Demeraran, followed
the Indian grandfather from Mauritius,

taking the younger sister to breed an heir,
a helix sprang which can't be boxed
in those grids with a man at the apex. All
continued marrying outwards. Her genes

encompass history and continents
in a luminous web in which are charmed
men with whom I have nothing in common
beyond our drinking together at weddings.

Request Slip

In the British Library,
rare book section, I was
served today knowledgeably
by a woman in hiding,
tented from head to foot
with a slit like a letter box
for studying my request slip.

I'm required to understand
why she needs this mask.
But my own mask of courtesy
needs something beyond
"my religion requires this."
Why, for the prophet's
sake? Would a glimpse

of your sardonic lips,
your hair like plaited tar,
have had me leaping
the enquiry desk to
press my suit on yours?
Lady, I withstand daily
assaults of cleavage,

lipstick and eyeliner,
the high buttock profile
of stiletto-heeled boots,
never relaxing the strict
rules of engagement,
and I share increasingly
your contempt for skirmishing.

Say I stood before you
shrouded, citing some
Mosaic commandment,
ordaining me asylum
from your unzipped
hormones, wouldn't you,
there in your *niqab*, giggle?

Those grey bearded
Ayatollahs, who veil
all your possible masks,
forget if they encased
you in some metal box,
atop an alabaster tower,
your voice would still allure.

The Matter

Fool, look in thy heart and write?
I've always preferred what's out there
(perceiving, yes, my angle of vision's
a problem, I'm no naïve Platonist),

but let's examine this heart business.
To begin with, how for sure do you
know it's there? I unbutton my shirt
and probe beneath my left nipple,

or above it, or a little to the right –
– dammit, the thing's not even
beating, it's my wrist reassures me,
feel it on the pulse, said Keats,

and that's closer to the bone for me,
who always needed the external
doorways, only afterwards discerning
from the poem the matter in my heart.

A Kind of Failure

That rarest of intellectual things
a wedding invitation,
Johnny and Jo, their beyond-
hope parents hoping
they'll indeed make a go
of it, the more lavish
the wedding, the more
binding the superglue;
so the bride's a cake
in her layers of icing,
with sugarplum attendants,
her groom the regulation
black-handled knife.

My son, my daughter,
if I bequeath you anything
as you try to buck the market,
my prayer is you negotiate
the difficult art of love,
knowing the voices against
are stronger than ever,
and a surviving marriage
is a kind of failure
(what's lacking in her
that she's happy with him,

what slavish devotion
is he basking in?).

At Ana and Paulo's,
even the priest, ebullient
in his jeans and surplice,
even the hippy priest, pulling
metaphors from the ropes
and anchor stonework
of his 500 year old
chapel, said: marriage
is like the *Carreira da India*;
of four carracks, risking
the Atlantic's winds and shoals,
only one returns cradling
rubies and peppers.

Voyaging is truly an aspect
of it, as are partner, lover,
passionate friend, live-in
helpmate, all the honourable
trite euphemisms that
yearn to reinvent love
and abolish property
in each other – appalled
by the flunky dictating
to the banquet hall
of Ascot hats
and hired penguins, *Be
Upstanding for the Bride*

in the macabre ante-chamber
of an English nuptial. Yet beyond
the *Country Life* position,

the vomit on the en suite
carpet, the jetlagged
honeymoon, our prayer,
Jo and Johnny, is
you find anchorage
in each other. May you
live to discover (like
the Tswana for whom only
lifetimes are short enough
to consummate a marriage),

the enduring words for your
voluntary roping are
indeed 'wife' and 'husband',
So let the skies rain
lark song from high
above the Quantocks,
and may the polluted
Severn be salmon-thronged,
then your estuary view
of Atlantic winds and shoals
will be only the normal
vicissitudes of lives
pregnant with happiness.

Birds & Bees for my Son

Today's women read two kinds of novel,
ending in marriage, starting with divorce;
to the former, you are still a mortgage with a garden,
to the latter, proof they can dispense with men.

You'll find your responsibilities laid down

by creatures ambitious to be themselves,
enacting their post-pill freedoms while you
must be selfless, monogamous and erect.

You could, of course, carry on as before,
much as they are doing now – playing the field,
turning the old double standard on its head. But
I promise you: there are rewards in choosing

a questioning woman and making it work.
You'll find they still have hearts, and I dare
affirm (with little experience of the other)
that, buoyed by friendship, the sex is better.

Fragment

.....You start
with a phrase that feels charged
in some way. It gives you a rhythm,
a tone, and if you're lucky, a sense
of the poem's shape. What
you don't know is what it's about.
You wait, as it pre-occupies you
days and nights, getting on with life,
your mind active all the time, cutting
the poem back to the bud, to its nouns
and verbs, the things named and what
they're doing, no room for superfluities,
the charge extending white-hot
through the wires of the poem's
self-assembly, and ending oddly
lucid. Then, for the first time,
you know joy .....

On the Train, Reading Dante.

Halfway along the line we have to travel
I found myself in a siding outside Doncaster:
the sky was darkening, the land was level.

Both sides were fields of industrial waste,
black water, derelict caravans.
To halt there and know the place exhausted

brought on the old despondence.
Nothing so fine as wolf, lion or leopard
(that's money, pride or concupiscence,

piquant temptations!) stood
in the track. Nor was I in control
the diesel waiting at red.

As when the slaver's musket barrel
flashed in the torchlight and the cave
grinned with its cache of skulls,

the faces of corruption came alive.
Nearest the mouth, Appetite
with a toadstool as hors-d'oeuvre,

wheeling its basket from the hypermarket
while the swollen-bellied, knob-
jointed world's children cry out.

Second skull, Theory, a spider's web
spun taut across the eye-holes:
mechanical and merciless its drab

dialectic. Next resident, Malice,
smirking from a ledge (what minister fixed
him there?) at blades and fibulas

scattered on the cave floor, a chalk wrist
reaching out, encircled by its amulets,
supplicating Treachery, Violence

and Fraud. I remember the clay pots
of millet beer, left in the entrance hole
to propitiate such malignant ghosts

as Dante Alighieri wrote to kill.
How thoroughly, without melodrama,
he marked down the lineaments of hell.

How solidly they live doing harm
to people who are known to me and I love.
Staring at my darkness I was calmer.

Then somewhere something happened, and I was moved.

Suleiman the Merchant

Night snow, what light it burns,
brighter than the wall, casting blue neon
up at a low sky radiant with lamps.
These colours are magic, we have changed
planets, pale grass, zebra trees,
shimmering orange clouds like a child's
or trader's vision or my own of purpose.

("Africa is a vast country," wrote Suleiman
the Merchant. "All the plants are black.")

Our Ninja Turtle Tuckboxes

With dusk it's still rising,
plumbing the walled oval between
ironbridge and stonebridge, creeping

up the black and white measure
by the hour. The crowd on stonebridge
simmers. This April night

the Zambesi's in York, trench-black
between owl-white ramparts, and we're
jubilant. Platoons of army and police

are larking about in boats with fireman's
hoists for leggy girls in mock
tournaments under Clifford's Tower.

The aerial drowned on King's Staith
is rumoured a BMW. After our fitted
kitchens, loft extensions, PCs

and cds, mountain bikes and Ninja
Turtle tuckboxes, we're
drunk with destruction. Floodlights

swirl in the mushroom eddies, hurtling
downstream like lava. Pubs
are standing room only, though

in the half silence that follows each
shout of the latest swallowed inches come
prickles of wonder at this

limestone egg, this camp luminous
with centuries of moonlight, this sliding
pitch, sleek with flashes like a crack

in the earth's crust. Here
was St William's miracle when woodbridge
tumbled and his swift intercession

revived from the tidewrack all
200 souls. Tonight, as
the pubs out, our future's present.

Lucy Poem

It always seemed there would be further
springs, the river in flood, moorhen
and primrose, curlew and wild daffodils,
after the revolution back to the celandine.

Those teaching this were my present age
then, ungratified, culpably eccentric:
after blood and drudgery there was mayflower,
this word being not nature but a text.

It isn't just pylons crossing the wheatfields
that puts the pastoral out of fashion:
whose heart can stop at a lagoon of bluebells
without feeling outdone in passion?

Always it seemed there would be fresh
innocence, the river in flood, otters
and coltsfoot, pigeons and wild honeysuckle,
after the revolution back to Dorothy.

The 11.56

The 11.56 daily from Paddington
to Gerard's Cross is a Parliamentary
train, not intended as a service.
Passengers are discouraged (it departs
from Platform 14), and tickets

must be cajoled. The carriages
are more than normally drafty,
buffet-less, the toilets dry.
No one intones *Mind the Gap*,
and no return is scheduled.

Across England such trains trundle,
7.26 daily, Polesworth to Crewe,
the cross-Wirral Helsby to Elsmere Port,
the Stalybridge Flyer, 9.22 Fridays,
or summer Saturdays, Frodsham to Runcorn,

along with stations, preserved
as in amber: Teeside Airport,
one passenger per week, Stafford's
Norton Bridge, with no foot access,
where the lamps come on eerily.

Cheaper by a quirk of governance
to keep open than to close,

these ghostly trains are scripted.
They bewitch us half-possessed,
duffle-coated acolytes,

into purposeless journeys – such
as this arthritic diesel mapping
Brunel's original genius,
past sidings overgrown
with buddleia, the collapsing

semaphore of wooden signal boxes,
the silenced morse of engine sheds,
while ticket collector Mohammed
is cheerful about his non-job,
"You're absolutely the first this week."
(adapted from *The Independent*, 1 December, 2014)

Resurrection

The doorbell rang. It was Jack, shorn
of his obituaries. I was dumb
with joy and Alice, hearing nothing, heard
something and rushed to embrace him.

After our tears, talk. There was money
and god, how proud I was there was money
and place. Beyond politics, beyond truth,
there was sanctuary for this driven family,

and my walk-on part in the dictator's fall
was ending with something done. I continued
as doorman-cum-secretary, harrowed
by glimpses of what I dimly guessed at,

bringing English insouciance to the abyss,
until one afternoon, two months on, I
passed him parked in a lay-by, scribbling
his first post-prison poem. And knew triumph.

The Highjack: an Epithalamium

1

The Boeing 707 highjack was in her
memory. He explained that precisely
through the intercom at Addis Ababa
with all the passengers still on board.
This was for her, his dead wife,
though the flight deck swam and terror
blanched his knuckles tightening on the grenade.

Refuelled, they flew on to Athens
where he released to her wine
and sunlight all but the flight crew
and the President. This was for
five years of her death in detention.
They simmered in the level glare,
the white terminal camouflaged by noon.

Terrorism, said the President coolly,
was a manageable crime. He owned
the banks and the plantations. They
had resources, it would take time.
The captain suffered, needing
action, not this messy politics.
At nightfall, the intercom sang with demands.

Justice! The negotiators groaned.
A lunatic! But the gunman had plans,
the International Court, councillors,
a mixed jury, the charge murder,
the President in the dock and three
governments pledging their honour.
Checking, they found him on their computers,

arrested in the Mall, frightening
horses during the state visit
with a starting pistol. A file
at the F.O., the naturalised wife
unprotected by her passport. Protest,
minutes, marginalia, the agreed text.
Crassly, the dead offer of compensation.

A Greek functionary had the idea:
the co-pilot was married and a steward
and one of the hostesses with sons.
That second night the thought climbed
hierarchies, and the man sympathised,
freeing the crew. So by morning, alone
with his enemy, he had saddened into error.

2

Full moon, guard her as she flies;
the air hungers
at such height: the cylinder
holding her is fragile:
no one knows what winds lurk
to whirl her into what spirals.

Full moon, as she flies, protect
from summoning desert,

swamp and jungle: ice
furs and clamps movement:
who can tell what armies wait
exacting what revenge from insult?

Full moon, shield her as she flies,
shine with superior
innocence on accident
and fevered malice: soot
seduces from the roof tops:
goddess, light her safely home.

3

Alone with his warder, the President
knew fear. In that hot tube,
foetid toilets, stench
thickening like smoke, it leaked
from his woollen banker's
suit, tie, silk shirt, underwear hand-
made, his trunk the source of corruption:
anything he unbuttoned, the smell was worse.

He knew why. He was powerless.
He envied his tormentor in slacks
and casuals such purity
of control. He had known it in jail
in the struggle when the sweet
odour seeping from the latrine bucket
was the air he lived on. He had smelt
it in countless others cowering at his feet.

Was the gunman's woman among
them? How could he know? Thirty
years he had studied

power, and seized it, and then
discovered how – that most things
happened beyond his knowledge. His orders
fluttered into swamps of incompetence
and rearing suddenly in ambush came events.

"I want", he muttered, "the latrine".
He heard his hoarseness and stumbled
to the first class toilet
squatting, with the door wedged open.
Latrine! This was power, to make him
talk like a poor man without thinking.
What had justice to do with this crouching
to ingratiate himself? Couldn't the whiteman

measure his absolute triumph?
Three days were enough to prove
him expendable. Others
would be trying out voices, there were
others the banks could appoint.
What remained was flesh, his guts
cramped with terror of the penalties
of pain the whiteman's power would exact.

4
She gave colour to cities: London
was slate or mousy, Lisbon
ten varieties of clay, and Athens
white, her gaze drawn always
upwards to the Parthenon.

She judged by restaurants: London
indoors, cloyed privacy, Lisbon
ten varieties of prawns, and Athens

where part of the fun was
visiting the kitchen.

Below the Acropolis she discovered
their *taverna*. How could
he live without her eye for design?
How let her death linger,
something capricious?

5

In the soft dusk shadows quickened.
He ran to the flight deck, shouting
down the intercom to pull
back their troops. They
swore faith but when he screamed
again they complied. He knew
they were waiting, out in the half light.
There was one enemy, and two
threatened: himself and his prisoner.

This wasn't the drug. He had made
a citizen's arrest, responsibly,
though his eyes ached
and he kept striding,
striding. Voices he ignored.
There wasn't a politician in the world
he would cross the street for, nor
policemen, nor the psychiatrist
whose honey drooled from the intercom –

Travelling they forgot colour.
Months went by innocently until
professionals made it
a symbol, heightening

his tenderness. Then they were
piano's black-and-white notes played
by? Soot seduced, the Parthenon glowed.
Oh Maria, yes, how she drew him
into her joyfully and gave absolution.

Tinker, tailor, beggar man, slave:
there was a frightened black man
to protect, poor
man. It was an error
letting the crew go free. No
politician cared about a black man
grey with fear. Gladly he lifted
and with love the weight of history
for his black wife and her murderer.

6

Beyond them all
was the forest
humming with spirits:
in a sunlit clearing
houses with reed
walls and plaited roofs,
and the farms
spreading like green lakes.

Beyond them all
was the river
with green islands
turning in the current:
on the river
paths at dusk
women slender
with water pots.

Cockcrow and children
and the husbands
planting, and wives
again to the river
as smoke unwound
from cooking fires.
In the forest
humming with spirits

crouched the hunter
with his charms:
duiker smooth
as an old hoe,
chimpanzee the drummer,
and buffalo before whom
unrequited the hunter
prostrates himself.

When they came
upriver by steamer
home, he was
ambushed by memory.
Within us all
is the forest,
the sunlit clearing
with houses and wood smoke,

self-sufficient,
the generations talking,
the circle unbroken
by travel or trade.
Innocence dies
hard in the lover
when forests advance
the spiked palisade.

7

So at midnight when the attack came
he was ready. He was standing
in shadow beside the open
hatch above the gleaming pond of the wing.
Moonlight through the cabin window
showed the President sleeping, shirtless.
Under the control tower vehicles
huddled. The attack, he knew,
would come from behind, the signal
voices from the flight deck to distract him.

No, he was not Hamlet the terrorist
nor Orestes. He had reached ends
and before him was
a wing like a column of moonlight on water.
I am Daedalus, he thought. I have
challenged heights. The voices came,
honeyed, mocking. He was startled,
alert. He heard two soft thuds
and feet running. The explosions merged
deafening as limpet charges blasted doors open.

Deliberately he stood in the moonlit
hatch and the first shot spun him,
falling in the silver
pool, rolling, sliding, dropping again,
embraced by the plane's black
shadow on the tarmac. Sirens
wailed, searchlights criss-crossed
above him and he heard his balked
attackers howling in confusion.
We have eluded them, he thought, and died.

That was the only ending. The President
rules for life. The women praise him
for conquering, his portrait
on their breasts. The bank's
crisp black-and-white notes print
his picture too, on the re-issue
after the devaluation, the new loan
paying interest on the old. Athens has
other highjacks. The marksman relishes
his Order of the Mosquito, second class.

3

On this Headland

On this headland of middle age and Europe
where the land ends and the sea begins
I write. October's rains are here.
Cicadas are shrilling in the pine trees,

and though swallows reckon this is autumn,
people are trooping to their allotments
with their Moorish over-the-shoulder hoes
to unlock the earth after the long drought,

and to one who, like Rilke, writes to correct
the mere accident of where I was born,
it's a swallow's instinct to resume
riding the waves of this place and time,

taking off from the edge, the gene
that propelled me half way round the world
to my *mestiço* muse, forging an idiom
in contradiction, from antipodes.

More Briefs

1

I put my pen down for a lunch of goat's cheese,
bread, last year's wine and a melon, looking out
across red-tiled terraces to fishing boats
back this morning hours before I bought bread watching
the groomed and ironed girls trooping lovely to the city
and came home to writing. Then a siesta,
a walk and writing. I am doing
what I should like to do for ever. No,

there will be no second stanza questioning
this. These and children and you blossoming
like morning glory on walls everywhere
are all a man could need, and paper. As for
the makers of bread and red wine, I would
trust them for life beyond the purveyors
of varnished cork tiles or fish tanks or plastic
flowers in the hypermarket on the Marginale.

2

"The most difficult art in the world," said
the *administrador* between mouthfuls, squid-prodding

fork raised, his right hand casting for the English words
(I thought of *ottava rima* and Camões)

"is the art of choosing a good melon."
Camões sits in his square under the pigeons:

his poetry is fired hard like tiles:
his round eye ridicules the end of empire.

To be fair to my friend (retired) the grilled squid
was succulent in the club where they planned the coup.

Everything that summer was like the wild melons
exploding at a touch to scatter seeds.

3

I parked outside the hospital in *Luis de Camões*
and waited. I was coaxing alive a poem.

Two men with a coffin went inside:
fifteen minutes later I had changed a tense.

Four men, two in tee-shirts, one with a cigarette,
shouldered the coffin into the hearse. The two stood back,

dusting nothing from their hands, easing their shoulders,
refusing thanks "for nothing", and crossed

the road to the café, ordering *aguadente*.
The poem clicked suddenly like a shut box.

4
Late summer brought Atlantic gales:
the beaches whitened, charcoal fires

flew wild. Behind our shutters we talked
suddenly of winter. Research

reveals, announced the team on TV,
there are 2229 basic Portuguese words.

Artur and his children came to dinner:
jailed by one side, exiled by the other,

he has been angered into cold action.
Afterwards at the window I ate grapes

spitting seeds into the swirling darkness.
Across the square under the flapping awning

a man and woman lingered over wine.

Coup, 1974

At last I find out
how to work the shutters:
people at the tram stop
look up at the noise
and wave back smiling.

There are posters
for May 1st: guns
and red carnations:
on the No Left Turn sign
a hammer-and-sickle.

A tram collects them
and sways downhill
between the tiled houses;
the smiles gather
to our room like doves.

Surfaces

(for Jill & Alberto Dias)

I like the cool tenor of tiles:

the coolest place in *Largo de Camões*
is the tile shop. More even than the *livrarias*,
dusty and cavernous with riches, it holds us.

There is the sea in tiles:

dolphins, wine-carriers, marketers, lilies,
discoverers and farmers,
are transfixed and transfigured

in a poetry of blue squares.

While the jangling trams snarl and gross fish
leer from the restaurant windows,
the houses are quiescent.
Tiles have burned their passions out:

they bring us back to surfaces, to dark wine,
a green bottle on a table cool with glaze,
afternoons of light and patterns:

tiles can be wiped clean endlessly.

The Narrowing Script

In front of the train's front seats, next
to the driver's cabin, with the same view,
is a fold down seat we evening commuters
jostle for, like school boys. Ours

is the fast train, skirting the estuary
the whole track to where the sun sinks
in the ocean. So close to the crashing
breakers is our tilt, the windows

crust with salt. Beach after beach
we see waders in their tribal feather.
The little boats and the golden girls
seem each man to his dream accessible,

though as eloquent are the Hornby points,
the rails' narrowing script, turned
Arabic by the spume. I sense this
journey plunging me back. And onwards.

Bacalhau

1

Another restaurant in Alcabideche! People
keep asking, "where's the new restaurant?"
and Alice directs them
confidently without having seen it.

Restaurants in Alcabideche are like
chapels in Wales. There is always some
new delicate doctrine
involving fresh coriander and salt cod.

At Christ's birth, codfish loom
on our TVs, glottal as Pavarotti,
roaring *Hark the herald* etc.
(The turkeys wilt and swoon.)

2

Bacalhau again! I found it
in Soho, but "it comes
from Hull" said Luigi, his
moustache quivering
at the absurdity: "they send
the heads to Portugal."

I hugged it under my elbow,
a brown paper rugby ball
in a neat net of string,
and set off across London.

At the F.O.
they were bombing Libya.
"One moment, sir".

"It's *bacalhau*," I said.
"Sir?"
"Salt dry cod."

Gingerly, he weighed the device,
gave it a gentle wobble,
smelt it and held it to his ear
listening to the music of the seas.

"Salt. Dry. Cod, sir?"
"They send the heads to Portugal
under the Treaty of Windsor".

He kissed the air and a dog,
special breed, tall
as the hat stand ambled
from the office, taking control.

My casket was offered knee high
like myrrh or frankincense
and I thought of the hundred recipes
simmering in the brown egg
    – *bacalhau*
      in the glorious names
    of Bulhão Pato, Gomes de Sá,
Batalha Reis, António Lemos,
Zé do Pipo and Brás.
    – *bacalhau*
    with cheese, with onions,
      with potatoes and spinach,
    with milk, rice, leeks, oysters,
    parsley, prawns, flour with egg white
    – *bacalhau* 'with everything'
      in the peasant style

with carrots
in the manner of heaven,
in twists like a corkscrew,
from Trás os Montes
       Guarda, Porto,
          Lamego,
             Ericeira,
                Alentejana, even
the despoiled Algarve,
and our winter favourite
       – *bacalhau que nunca chega,*
          "the cod that's never enough" –

I watched them hatching in the dog's
nostrils, clamouring
to spawn in the cold seas
of their birth.
                (Ghadafi'd
have surrendered on the instant,
adding his own touch
of tabina and walnuts.)

The Alsation took a quarter sniff
turning its tail contemptuously.
Cook, poet, comedian,
I was harmless.
Our government's in safe paws.[1]

---

[1] (Alice White faults this poem for not including *Bacalhau á moda
da Guida*, as prepared by Margarida Maria da Cruz Mergulhão of
Vila Verde, Figueira da Foz.)

The Last Arab

The last, mournful Arab in Obidos
is an Englishman, a contract manager,
in love with Portugal but, above all
else, admiring things properly run.

– as when the Moors managed the Lagoa
as a seaway, right to the citadel's
western precipice, a shimmering
haven (as he will conjure it for you)

scything inland, matching beauty
with purpose, every centimetre farmed
for eels and oranges, corn and olive oil,
and governed by experts with eyes alert

to the brown silt descending the rivers
and the sand bar's linked architecture:
the citric, dawn wail of the muezzin,
the poetry of water, sun and rock.

Knife-Grinder with Pigeons

The sea today's a blue razor. Senhor
Campos' pigeons are making their morning tour
of inspection. Watering flowers

I freeze at that music, jug upturned.
Five notes, those wooden
pipes! It's our knife-grinder

peddling one-handed. We hear him

twice monthly and each time, time
stops. But the man's more dreamer

than craftsman. Give him your best
breadknife, he returns it
an obscene spike in his quest

for an edge that will slice
a hair standing. He's that most dangerous
of citizens, a perfectionist.

Listen! How many
rings can there be
to a five-note change? Yet he

never repeats. Each phrase unfurls
rising or falling, complete in itself,
plaintively different. The pigeons twirl

above the bay's glare, for whole seconds
invisible as they bank in unison,
reappearing lumpily like a squadron

of amateurs with two panicking
to catch up. Those haunting notes.
They make your neck's

hairs stand. So many
worlds are mourned by this man, such fallen
civilisations, such golden

ages tarnished. Again,
perfect! It brings tears
to the eyes. People are running

out with their knives. The bay shatters
like a windscreen. Water crusts
in my jug. But the crystals

are of laughter. They are joking
down there, begging back
their scissor spikes

from their hectic musician
who is grinning through his perspiration
"por favour, just one more revolution".

* * * * *

Senhor Campos' pigeons have collected
their flutterings homewards. Their *kru-kruing*
is like a dream of the domestic

(again those five notes, from the next *bairro*).

The Three Graces

In dusty tomes at the back of *livrarias*
or on tiles in the loveliest of the old palaces,
they are still there, the Three Graces,
Portuguese, Indian and Brazilian Negress,

embracing or in triptych, each displaying
all but one of her charms and proffering
gifts, the apple, the mango, the pawpaw,
while around them curve the appropriate

fronds of banana, palm and olive branch.
They celebrate possession, the fruitfulness
of a bankrupt empire. They are three Eves
with the appropriate serpents, Man's fate

on three continents. But who is not charmed
by their sisterhood? Each is different
but perfect. They let us dream innocently
of universal love (at least among womankind).

Antonio Rui

Antonio Rui whose township mother was always,
grinned the white managers, available
                                      if you were desperate,

Rui, born in the *bairro*, father unknown,
with a cleft palate, a game leg, and sore
                                      corrupting his eardrums,

would hobble the track between tin-roofed shanties
where women sweated at mortars, or dragged behind them
                                      huge water barrels,

with a watch strapped to his left wrist, a transistor
clapped to his right ear, gold teeth smiling, his shades
                                      reflecting coconut palms,

and jabbering, stammering in tortured Portuguese
of a Grundig next year, a Suzuki, an outboard motor,
                                      a Boeing 747 to Lisbon,

and we shared the joke. What worked and gleamed

he worshipped. People being flawed irreparably, polished
                              gadgets were his icons.

Today, years on, earphones, Grundig, digital watch,
we met him hobbling in *Largo de Camões*, as voluble
                              with images as ever:

next year he will cross the Tagus, next year
a beach house for his mother, next year the white men
                              will make him *chefe*.

The Little Boats

Early morning, from the fast train,
the little boats faced upstream
in the polished-pewter estuary,
straining at their buoys.

Late afternoon, in the glowing bay,
the painted boats faced out to sea,
the U of their limp hawsers slitting
tarmac Vs in the liquid gold.

Poetry of Verandas
(for Helen and Hélio Álves)

1
Here's evening, pinesmoke
with shafts of gold,
the sheer well-being
of a mosquito bite.

On the third floor up we are
up among birds, not
the caged canaries but
martins veering so
tight I could grab them
like Jehengir Khan who caught
the swallow at Lords.

In the haze, a pigeon
stutters by, anxious
and out of his depth.

Come, poetry,
smoulder, lascivious
as charcoal, target
the ear like senhor mosquito,

zoom like the martin's
shadow, skimming
tessellated pavements, leaping
houses, somer-
saulting, can
turn on an *escudo,*
is most feigning
in its scything graphite
when closest to matching
the uncatchable.

2

For Luís Vaz de Camões, then, how was it
quarantined just down there off Cascais
all-but-home after seventeen Christmases
the plague raging, Lisbon a necropolis,

112

how did he feel the colonial voyager
with his vision of Portugal, his *octavo*
epic sundried and nurtured through
mutilation, fevers and shipwreck

in the bag? Was the court corrupter
than he recalled, the clergy more ignorant,
the boy king distinctly odd? Had he
second thoughts about the Moor?

And was his stop-press dedication impassioned
or politic? *Sebastian, my King, Guarantor*
of our Ancient Liberties, born to extend
the Empire of the Faith ... (a case of poetry

making something happen? Disaster!)

3
Summer long
on all the beaches, children
sculpture in sand
the Discoveries:

anchors, caravels,
Henry the Navigator,
Adamastor
of the Cape of Storms.

Summer long
on all the beaches, the sea
salt with tears of Portugal
swills them away.

4

I'm still wondering about Camões, having
myself (to compare great things with small)
been seduced overseas by visions of home
as a place where matters were better organised

and returned to the grim reality. Thatcher
was not unlike Sebastian, and the Falklands
turned on a coin. Now we are hoist
with myths of greatness betrayed, and I recall

the honourable old man at Belém cursing, as
the caravels waited, *this lust for gold,*
this ambition to be lords of India, Persia,
Arabia and Ethiopia, this cruel ferocity

with its philosophy of death. Camões
invented him and gave him eloquence, but
the north wind swelled the sails (as it did)
and nothing could undo the vast event

(which the poet, as true historian, marvelled at).

5

And here he's again, the Father
of Winds. Our matted pines
heave like an ocean, the almond trees

fuss prettily, ancient olives
munch and fumble, blue gums
bunch their shadow-boxing fists,

while up on the skyline, royal palms
semaphore with their ostrich feathers
to clouds scudding like clippers

on the Azores run. The Atlantic's
in every blast, and how
the swallows pinion it, cruising

under our block's cliff, accelerating
in the domestic air, hitting
the corner, and

FLAWEWEWEWEWE they are puffballs, ounces
of cartilage, sheer as silk to spattering
on the tessellated pavements,

feathering at the last split-
second in a teetering
pole-vault, swooping, skimming

the perfected charcoal of their shadows.
I watch them
trying on wings. I watch them

readying for the dangerous currents south.

Moon Talk

Each full moon, swimming at dusk
above the ridge where dawn
dawns, is a reckoning. How
has your month been spent?

Its red, quizzical face questions
intimately. What are you about?
Where are the poems you could have written?
How many hours have you given to love?

It peers like a Chinese grandmother
cracking her knuckles. What have you
done for your children? To which
ancestors have you poured wine?

Each desert, earth-bound moon,
tilting in the sun's reflected
light, asks, Where in the world
are you going? There is no other.

Let me tell you, Jack …
(for, and after Jack Mapanje)

Let me tell you, Jack, what's beyond the veranda
Where I write most days, except when the north wind
Blasts from York across Biscay to ravage
Our pottery garden of the plants you know from home
– Hibiscus, elephant ears, Mary's milk, *piri-piri*.

I've lost count of the half poems launched to probe
For metaphors to enshrine what's out there. *Enshrine!*
Don't giggle! Obsolete words, like *enamelled*
Or *the painter's palette*, invade them for colours no one
Younger than 50 in England has ever exclaimed at,

And you know well enough I don't just observe
From a height. I'm down there daily, like Wordsworth
In the gap between stanzas, peering short-sightedly

At silks thrusting from the earth, and interrogating
Passers-by for the word, though they often don't know.

So my diary is of distances, of fragments and hesitations,
About white walls daubed with laundry and geraniums,
About the moss-green valley, where nettles even in winter
Surge knee-high, and snakes fat as pythons coil in the sun.
Pine trees cast shadows blacker than Alentejo bulls,

And spring's sequence of flowers is like a carpet somehow
Lit from within, changing not by the month or the week
But hourly between daybreak and noon and dusk
As the massed gold or china-blue or tortoiseshell petals
Open, revolving with the blossoming sun, and fold and decline.

I watch the cat boxing her kittens. Boys yelp like peacocks.
Cocorico happens too often to be any use as a clock.
Oh, but laugh at this! Our morning parade, as housedogs
Walk their mistresses, each circumscribed by her territory
Marked by a tree, a lamppost, and a raised hind leg.

You would hardly know the Atlantic is just a kilometre
Off, until the stump of a hurricane howls from New York
And the rain clouds scud like caravels, their hulls
Careened by the moon. Skies are important here, stars
In their consternations, flagging imperial destinies,

So I use you as reference point, your well-being differently
Based, knowing our love (another jaded word, with its
Dangerous afterlife) will survive this latest exchange
Of countries and poems. This valley beyond my veranda
Is my newest mystery, my second-hand Brazil,

Where I'm less ex-patriate than in York. Out there

Between the almond trees and blue-black cypresses
Is a field of flowers where the Angolans are playing football.
Language will come. I want to continue living
Where I will always marvel at precisely where I am living.

The Instinct

1

A third of a century ago I knew Lal,
a thin, brown man with high cheek bones
and evasive slits for eyes. For a while

we were friends, though with little in common
beyond Slim, his brother-in-law's steelband
which filled my days then, along with a woman

I had partly forgotten until I remembered Lal.
He was somehow special for being no one,
just Lal, no surname, jobless, no definable

Portuguese, Indian, Chinese or African
symptoms, just an end-of-line everyman
occupying earth. I met him once with a bin

of shoes he was trashing in the storm drain.
Neighbours had paid him to heel them. Ditching
the drumfull, he was ready to start again.

That's all I knew of how he made his living.
"Sometime," he said of the shoeless, "I does
really wonder if they know what they doin'."

But in just one line of his life, hunched
over a tenor pan clawed from an oil drum
tempered in a furnace of tyres, its notes punched

out with a sawn-off six-inch nail, Lal
was the sweetest of perfectionists. No one
could double-wrist a purer, silkier drum roll,

more violin than percussion, from the piano-toned
ring of fifths round the pan's circumference,
nor beat from the off-pitch silver medallions

of the dustbin's shrill concave, tighter scales
or more intricate arpeggios in what he termed,
wryly as I arranged them, "heavy classics".

He brought, far more than me to this craft
of poetry, six hours nightly practice.
He was a man who taught me and, before I left,

                    .

I made him, along with Midnight, Wayne, Smokey,
Slim, Scorpion and the band, just one,
ambiguous gift, an American tour. Disembarked,

he vanished conclusively into that vacant heaven.

2

Years afterwards, in another language,
in an African village so obscure
she had to borrow a wrap to meet me,
I met with Emily Makua.

Her wuthering name showed Britain
had some priestly hand in her past,

part redeeming, part embellishing
but abandoning her at last.

Even the cloth she borrowed
was a third-hand Java print.
She lived beyond the periphery
of where money's made and spent.

Approaching her was a *rite de passage:*
at the ford, discarding my shoes,
I was too soft to continue barefoot
(my companions couldn't choose).

She was wizened yet articulate,
a widow with nothing to hide.
She spoke of her eleven babies,
nine of whom had died.

Being Christian, she refused to talk
of witches, or blame her husband:
being respectful, she cast her life
in the third person plural of custom.

A sleeping mat, a pot, a ladle,
a corner of somebody's hut:
I had met no other human being
so utterly destitute.

I sat on the chair they brought me,
she knelt on the beaten mud floor.
I asked about maize, cotton, rubber, tobacco:
she wouldn't agree she was poor.

She repeated a story I had heard
inattentively elsewhere,
about a barren woman who coaxed and moulded
a baby from a cucumber.

When her neighbour's children ate it,
she was taken up to heaven
and offered two clay pots, one new,
still eddying from the oven,

the other cracked and blackened
by years of household fires:
she warmed to it, and from it leapt
the child of her desire.

Back home, her neighbour envied her:
heaven gave her equal treatment:
she chose the flawless pot and flames
consumed her on the instant.

Such tales have little resonance
when reported by my peers:
from such a person in such a place
it moved me to tears.

3

These I write of were never my audience
(how could I hope to speak to them?)
but in fashioning experience

they became touchstones for a poetry
plain as an oil drum or cooking pot,
chastened by fact, scorning hyperbole

and all unreflecting metaphor, but an art
capable of such transformations
as the agile wrist or the heart's

yearning of those (never the 'other') reduced
to nothing or to no one, can kindle
summoning words and music.

I trusted on such evidence speech,
sure as whatever guides the swallow
or propels salmon to their home reach,

to keep us human, re-inventing
the aboriginal word made flesh
(with reference to our necessary closure).

Minerva's Cure

Gathering olives (Minerva's gift,
to rein in Neptune's foaming
stallions), dragging down
olive branches and plucking the black

bitter pearls, I feel as ancient
as the human race. How many down
millennia have performed these reaches
since some greater genius than the first

wheeler-dealer with his souped-up
sledge, found learning, subtlety,
all the arts of eloquence in these
astringent pips, these goat-droppings?

Olives should be, of course, a matter
for the village, with spread sail-cloth
and an army of beaters, not this
ex-pat with a *Jumbo* bag, but I'm

content to be the last to farm
this abandoned oliveira, relishing
each silver-smithied leaf, each
bough lichened with age, as shook

olives tumble down my shirtfront
and my hand purples with juices.
I plan to follow Minerva's cure (being
harmless never harmed a soul).

Massamba with the Brilliant Flowers

(i.m. Luiza Drennon, 1924-91)

1

After the mass in her memory when her daughters
Prayed for her journeying soul
In the village she knew only from their letters

To Africa, we gathered to eat the meal
She would have cooked for her sons-in-law,
Massa, massamba and, squatting by the charcoal

Brazier with a tumbler of smoky Portuguese *Dão*,
Two peppered chickens spiked like crucifixes,
Shrugging off with an indignant "Chi-sá"

Any male offers of help as she licked

The knife and pronounced them done.
This was five thousand miles ago, a far cry

From the white-robed daughters of Zion
Singing of chariots swinging low, of the roll call
Yonder she had answered in heaven

With rest beyond Jordan for her ransomed soul.
These were the hymns of her comfortless years
Making one daughter a stranger at her funeral,

Weeping with the singers but preferring a mass
For the mother whose disappointments were catholic.
She died God's orphan, a cantankerous

Wanderer. She lost every trick
As power's colour changed round her. Every rule
She bent to – child marriage, the black

Face of poverty and labour – every accommodation failed
As her places failed her, leaving her
Grieving over the twins, divorced, with the rebels

On the city road and flight across the border
Her Rock of Ages refuge. So, after the blessing
Of the Host and the Benedictus, we gathered

Sadly with salt and maize flour for our own *massa,*
Pre-packed from the hypermarket on the *Marginale,*
And two chickens from the factory spiced

With her paste of lemon, pounded pepper and garlic,
With beers on ice, the charcoal tinkling,
The sons-in-law subservient to her liking,

And *massamba* begged from the *quinta*
In the dry lagoon of old Senhor Palmiro
Who was bemused by these exotics from Moçambique

Hovering like butterflies along his furrow,
Picking pumpkin leaves to be steamed with coconut,
With tomatoes, onions and the brilliant flowers,

And blossoming at the table in three of her daughters,
Each of them taller in unconscious mime,
Chafing in the households she had nurtured

And pilloried, bewitched and bewitching as her prime.

2

December's end. The kitchen half-door
swings open on the bulb-lit yard where
rain is drifting like firework
smoke, like the spray of a windblown

waterfall into our yellow
pond of lamplight. Below is a sprig
of mottled green-and-off-white
ivy, waxed like a tree frog.

Beyond, in the dark tank of moonless
starless midnight, sleek
buds of the flowering currant
are luminous as tropical fish.

So the year ends in blessedness,
a festering family quarrel
healed, a dear friend
resurrected from the living death

of the camps, the old words printed.
Out there, in the mild night under
soil under the fine rain,
tubers and roots stir quietly

of crocuses, cornflowers,
irises and blue geraniums,
tulips and nasturtiums,
lilies, foxgloves, the poppies' brilliant

unsteady silks,
reliable as night and day
with their calendar of beauty,
are out there, stirring

in the darkness
under the fine spray,
while she for whom we grieved
this year in the grim void

of her going, stirs
now in our hearts more calmly
with thoughts of her good
years, the satires we repeat

at table, lovingly, laughingly, sharing
her with our friends, bequeathing
pride to our half-listening
sons off-stage who,

barely remembering her, wear
her mark as we do. She swung
open my heart to simplicity
by her death with its quiet beginnings.

126

Letter to My Son

I am fifty years old
    and writing to you from high summer.
Wheat fields from the hollow
    to the swelling horizon
Have been combine-scythed
    in swirling parallel strokes.
There are swallows up here
    clicking in African languages.
Black cattle wading
    in the shadows of olive trees
Are barely visible
    so black are the shadow pools.
Cicadas among the cornflowers
    are sawing at their washboards
(A linking image from my '50s bored
    teens to your own, as

Suddenly articulate
    you start your own journey).
Whatever I can give you
    has long been given if at all.
There's little more you will
draw on beyond occasional cheques.
    But I want to write of my love
for you over seventeen winters,
    Both the barren anxiety
that shadows your present choices,
    And my pride in you
and your emerging designs
    Like a carnival of poppies
crowding the disturbed soil
    Of motorway embankments
with their gift of summer.

Update from a Distant Friend

(Zomba to Blantyre, after Jan Kees Van Donge)

"Their uniforms were new to me, shimmering
Pink and purple, and so was their elation.
At the hospital stop they commandeered
The all-but-empty bus and I thought them
Kitchen orderlies or the like from, maybe,
Thondwe, but we humped the bridge
Luminous at dusk and they stayed on board
Joking like people with an explosive secret.

"Night fell and we clattered the tarmac
In our yellow tunnel between darkness
And the blue gums. The furred hills
To the west bristled against the sky's
Slashed purple and pink, and every
Five kilometres or so an estate house
Radiated wealth in this land of silenced
Villages. At the Magomero turn-off

"I was drawn with my halting chiChewa
Into their talk. Who were they? Where
Were they going? This fired guffaws
And head-wagging with a mutual
Slapping of palms, and this riddle:
Who travels without travelling to?
Slave who's impregnated the chief's
Wife! Hunter with buffalo in his path!

"At Njuli, they'd a new one for me:
Who counts up instead of counting down?
We reached the firelit shacks of the first
Squatter camps, then the first township,

And I tried to imagine these landless people
Mounting instead of sliding. But I was
In the wrong market. *It's the detainee.*
They told me, *not the sentenced prisoner.*

"And that was their tale. Freed that day
To honour the Dictator's brain surgery,
Held while the unlucky rioted (two dead),
Then smuggled out in their pink and purple.
The man sharing my seat had done 24 years.
When we reached the depot with no onward
Buses that night, I was emotionally
Broken at the gap between their lives and mine."

Breakfasting with Bees

Autumn, I breakfast with the bees
up here not for the flowers but the sun.
An hour after dawn, it breaks
hot and gold above the ridge opposite,

descending our boxed verandas
like a blow torch, and the bees hover
in full orchestra on invisible threads
of air, as mist burns off in the valley.

Then the dancing begins, in dizzying
spirals of ecstasy. I sit motionless,
breath suspended as three alight
on my arm and forehead, combing

their legs, then off again in helter-
skelters of frenzy. It's done, before

my coffee has cooled. They depart
without deflowering my felicias.

The Most Deceiving

Fernão Mendes Pinto. Viva!
memorialised in the famed *Thesaurus*
as *conjurer, deceiver, liar,*
trickster, humbug, a massed chorus

of *Pharisee, Rosicrucian, Jesuit,*
actor, jobber, dissembler, charlatan,
all because you refused to credit
the Portuguese could civilise Japan!

In your book, the pious Catholic
pirate, ruthless as any infidel,
bound by his imperial ethic
rapes, despoils, betrays, kills.

You mock yourself as God's missionary
lampooned for eating with your hands.
How could you not go down in history
but as by-word for the *soi-disant?*

Medicaster, saltimbanco,
I hope in Dante's whichever hell
jockey, perjurer, Cagliostro
Roget's doing time for libel.

My question's this: as you ploughed
old memories into your jeremiad

blockbuster *Perigrinação,*
did you know of C. and his *Lusíads?*

While the picaresque and satiric
danced from your goosequill in Almada,
the sublime and truly epic
went begging in Alcântara,

the briefest of river trips apart,
within hailing distance as it were.
Did you never share a heart-to-heart
with that other Eastern warrior?

Your buccaneers were his *barões.*
He saw God's designs turning
on the deeds of mariners you disowned
and reckoned fit for burning.

Two masterpieces, alternate visions,
divided by an estuary
which drifts into the setting sun,
that uncompromising referee.

You won your case, you lost your cause,
for history's unkind to truth,
bestowing all her best applause
on those capable of myth.

It's no unflattering epitaph
to be yoked with the most deceiving,
Luís de Camões' apocryph,
and an author to believe in.

Xmas Dinner

Our recipe starts ruthlessly, *Mata-se*
O leitão (kill the piglet) *com um golpe*
Na goela (with a sharp blow to the throat)!
All feasts begins with a death, but who capable

Of doing this needs to read how to do it?
And which of us ex-patriates could accomplish
Such an act? Could pretty Odette
(Who wrote our cookbook) do it? Does she

Require it of her husband? This is no
Recipe, but an elegy for a vanished
Portugal. Picture, it tells us, the tiny
Backyard in the cobbled street of whitewashed

Cottages, among the pruned vineyards
Of Bairrada, where the piglet you feast on
Was bred at your hands, and manhood
Knows what's its due and what's due to woman.

Odette concludes, *Borrifa-se* (use a spray
Of parsley) to sprinkle the piglet
Generously with white wine. So picture me,
Kneeling on the kitchen floor, attempting it.

The Cormorants

Around the island in the midday glare
a dozen sooty cormorants drift.
They never alight. At times, one plunges
without creasing the estuary's mirror,

and ascends, vanishing at cliff height, where
above the loaf-shaped island in the heat
a dozen white gannets spiral. You
can barely see them, until one veers

and sunlight glints on its bright plumage
as its twin plunges. For there are no
cormorants, only the gannets' shadows
wheeling in the noon's distraction.

What labours within the green inlet
will never mate with the flopping heron.
The swallow skimming the River Douro
leaves its image dissolving as it soars.

October's Sickle Moon

(for Abu Zeide Mohamede Ibne Mucana)

*(The pull of the soil was always very strong for the
Andalusian poets who, for the most part, were of country
origin ... Such was the case of Ibne Mucana al-Isbuni.
Having lived at Seville at the court of the Abbadides, then at
Grenada at the court of Zirides, he knew the inanities of the
courtier's life and relinquishing the bogus fame of the royal
salons he returned to his village of Alcabideche, close by
Sintra, to end his life cultivating his field. "I saw him" said*

133

one of his fellow countrymen who recounted to Ibne Bassam
his encounter with the old poet, now deaf, his sickle in his
hand. "I approached him and when I had taken him by the
hand he made me sit down to look at the field ... I asked him
to recite some poetry and he improvised.")[2]

1

"Dwellers at al-Qabdaq, husband well your seeds
    whether of onions or pumpkins.
A man of purpose needs a windmill turning
    with the clouds, not with water.
Al-Qabdaq doesn't produce, even in a good year,
    more than twenty sacks of corn.
Any more than that, the wild pigs come down
    from the forest in regular armies.
She is meagre with anything good or useful,
    just like me, as you know, I have a poor ear.
I abandoned the kings in their finery, I refused
    to attend their processions and parted from them.
Here you find me at al-Qabdaq, harvesting thorns
    with my sharp and agile sickle.
If someone said, "Is it worth this trouble?"
    you'd answer, 'The noble man's ensign is freedom'.
Abu Bakr al-Muzaffar's love and good deeds were my guide
    so that I left for a garden in springtime."

2

We meet the old deaf poet with a sickle, crofting
The northern border of a country whose south

---

[2] From the French of Henri Peres: Abu Zeide Mohamede Ibne
Mucana, eleventh century Andalusian poet; Aby Bakr al-Muzaffar,
Prince of Badajoz, d. 1068.

Is the River Senegal. He has turned his back on
Kings in their finery, comparing men of purpose
With windmills, circling with the clouds, not
Water – though we may be sure these rains, after
The scorched weeks of house-repairs and weddings,
This season of the pumpkin and onion seeds he
Celebrates in his poem, when olives ripen and lamplike
Oranges burnish the quick dusk at the Call to Prayers,
We may be sure October's crocuses are a sign.

He lives when the Straits open on nowhere, perilous
To sailors pitched west in the inland sea but
No border. After the drought, October's rains.
Then the winds blow from Guinea and heat returns.
For him, this is Morocco and ordinary. The world
Is neither Europe nor Africa. These slopes of heather
And copper bracken, these drifting wine-coloured
Leaves as the swallows gather on whatever in his
World are telephone wires, they speak of the rains.
Then the golden windfall oranges tumble among
Daffodils, signalling harvest and another season

Building families. He has two fears: the wild boars
From Sintra mountain, foraging through his corn
In packs, and Portugal, the kaffir north. Rightly,
For we came and took purchase. Today, after
Autumn's virginal crocuses and the swallows' flight
South, our chestnuts blaze every colour of Fall.
We have baptised his seasons (*Por São Martinho,
Prova teu vinho*), and ceased believing. His poem's
Year's a calendar we have forgotten. Our cliffs
Bristle with immigration patrols. His stone windmills
Are chic retirement homes for the circling rich.

Yet dawn brings walls of morning glory, houses
Shining at jigsaw angles, the oliveira's feather-
Light windmill, the church on the mound where
Water, which explains all, still springs from the rock.
All day our houses soak up sun, surrendering
Colour, storing heat in a stunned precision of light
And shade. Over-exposed, even the windmill falters.
Beyond everything, the Atlantic's razor blade.
Our dusks are green wine. In the windmill's spinning
Penumbra, olive trees smoulder. Houses blaze
Separate textures. The dry-stone cabbage allotments

Glow like skylights, where we encounter the old
Poet extemporising in strict metre his satires
On the wretched soil of his birthplace. He has
Abandoned processing with kings. He has brought
To this onion patch Aristotle and Galen, turning
At each line's end to complete the couplet.
He husbands seeds. He grinds with the wind,
Spinning the cog-wheeled poetry of his freedom
In this all-man's-land, neither Europe nor Africa.
Tonight, as October's sickle moon sprints
Through marbled rain clouds, his windmills sigh.

Just Fine

Ridiculous, a year this side of sixty
to be sitting on the veranda over the garage
worrying she is an hour late, as though
I were still twenty with a teenager's

tangle of emotions and a young husband's pride.
But dusk is closing on our customary sun-downer

and my heart kicks at the thought of the message
that must one day far too early come

about her to me or about me to her
in no pidgin I will understand or signs
in any way bearable. I know from its vowels
that is not our Rover rounding the corner

nor her whine of deceleration, yet I stare
down all the same just as the phone screams
and it's okay, she's at her sister's, yes of course,
until ten, of course, yes, everything's fine.

Do Tempo Perdido
(after Sebastião da Gama)

Before we left I watched for two hours
darkness closing on our golden beach.
It began with the cliff's shadow

sliding along the bright sickle, touching
the bathers and the lovers who rose
separately and dressed. It stretched

out across the emerald waters so
clear you could stare
down fifty metres and see

the fishing boats silhouetted
on pale sand. You could see mackerel
hovering and the drifting tresses

of water plants. Then darkness clicked

and the sea became only the mirror
of an olive sky and of lights flickering.

I watched for an hour the colours
of that surface. Perfection
and effort and error

are a loss beyond irony.
I could see houses and the fishing boats,
whitewashed and pantiled, or painted

every colour, giving out lights
all present in the poem
of the sea's surface, and defeated.

Olive became pewter, hardening
to blacklead, and still
the oil murmured.

I asked for the bill
and you wrote a cheque
and we struck the steep hill

into the night without speaking.
From the summit
the sea was a void, beckoning.

Lamps in old vineyards
blessed our hurtling
down converging valleys to our bed.

From Episode in a War

2

Swamp and corrugation. She was not meant
to be outside. Five days they kept her
drugged in the customs house in the delta.
She lay on a white sheet in a cotton shift.
Five noons shimmered the island to sepia
squinnying her pupils though her blue eyes stared.
She was grounded metres above the river.
At dusk, husbanded impatiently, she watched
evening wrecked on a reef of coconut palms.
Day six, Ernesto shrank from his pale wife
getting drunk in a village near Mathilde
where satirical women opened their blouses
to give suck to the white man. That evening
she walked in her white shift to the beach.
Rust and detritus, the channel gouged
between hulks, the jetty a swamped freighter,
foredeck clutched by hands of mangrove, hold
bottomless with writhing embryos it had
dizzied her to stare down as she disembarked
while, sunk around her on the beach, sand
combed through her languid fingers was rust
of bolts, rivets, pipes, boilers, anchors,
buoys, steel plates, hinges, flaking, crumbling
like driftwood, dissolving. Clouds blazed
above the coconut flags. A dugout fought
the current with ringing solo and undertow
from six chanting paddlers. Flashes of pink
were flamingos returning. The first mosquito
she stamped her name ISOBEL on the white sand
in the high tide slick where banana roots,

oil seeds, clumps of water hyacinth reeked
of reeds upriver where he forgot her baby.

4

Ernesto woke with a headache on the mud floor.
He was going to beat that woman. He knew
what the terrorists did to Moises Ernesto.
They tossed him on their bayonets. They played
volleyball on the lawn with his little head.
He was a man. He had to exist knowing
such things. But she? A man needed comfort
when his baptised son was murdered, not
this deafening with silence. Go back
upriver? Fighting the current with the green
ambush waiting and the boy already dead?
His Excellency the Governor said, "Ernesto,
condolences, you did well to save the launch."
He was going to punish that woman. Not
tell her, that would be cruel. Only men
lived with knowledge. But teach her duty
like this woman with water from the river
and a rag to wash his prick and firewood
to roast his breakfast of mealie cobs – he
pulled her on top of him and rolled her over
and fucked her as she grumbled about children
and daylight. Well, she'd reason. He paid
extra. He enjoyed it more anyway, buying
these days.

　　　Walking home under coconuts
in the amber slatted light, he cursed
marrying her cotton chastity, remembering
the breasts of the mother of his sons.
They were all he had now. They weren't bad
kids, the little devils, and their mother's

breasts and her brown compliance – why
had he left them to marry this Portuguese?
Why, *por deus* had he spent his savings on
a wife from Vila Nova with her cold silence?
His boys were all he had now. He would
teach them volleyball, give them *his name*!
He walked on in wonder, his boot prints
crushing on the sand the marks of hundreds
of bare feet. Nothing had ever satisfied
like this revenge. A landrover honked
behind and he hitched a lift from a grinning
black corporal. "You kill any terrorists?"
"*Sim*, bwana. Three by the bridge this shining
morning. *Viva unidade! Viva the Republic*!"

4

Bounty

seamen (hung Spithead); Peter Heywood, midshipman (guilty
but pardoned) and William Muspratt, assistant cook
(acquitted on technicality); John Mills, gunner's mate, and
Isaac Martin and Alexander Smith, alias John Adams, able
seamen (d. Pitcairn Island); Joseph Coleman. Armourer,
Thomas McIntosh, carpenter's crew and Charles Norman,
carpenter's mate (acquitted on Bligh's testimony).

Prescript: Landfall

HMS Dolphin: 1767

June 20: At 9 A.M. we was oblidged to laye to,
espetially as we heard the sea Bracking and making
a great notice on some reefs of Rocks. In a short time
the fogg cleared up, and we now suposed we saw
the long wishd for Southern Continent so often
talkd of, but neaver before seen by any Europeans.
The country had the most beautiful appearance its
posable to Imagin, with great numbers of trees with
flowers of various colours which must certainly bear
some sort of fruit yet unknown to us – but I shall drope
this Discourse as no good spy Glass discovered it to me.

We saw upwards of a hundred canoes betwixt
us and the brakers all padling off towards the ship.
When they came within pistol shot they lookt at our ship
with great astonishment, and padled round and made
signs of friendship to us, holding up Branches of Plantain,
and uttering a long speech of near fifteen minutes.
Some of the sailors Grunted and Cryd lyke a Hogg
then pointed to the shore – oythers crowd Lyke cocks

to make them understand we wanted fowls.
This the natives of the country understood and Grunted
and Crowd the same as our people, and pointed to the shore
and they brought a good many fine young Girls down
of different colours, some was a light coper colour oyrs
a mulatto and some almost if not altogeather White –
This new sight Atract our mens fance a good dale,
and the natives observed it, and made the Young Girls
play a great many droll wanting tricks, and the men
made signs of friendship to entice our people ashoar.
All the sailors swore they neaver saw handsomer made
women in their lives, and declard they would all to a man,
live on two thirds allowance, rather nor lose so fine
an opportunity of getting a girl apiece – even the sick
which hade been on the Doctors list now declard
a Young Girl would make an Excelent nurse and they
were Certain of recovering faster under a Young Girl's
care nor all the Doctor would do for them.

                                        All this time
the Bay was lined round with men, women and children,
to see the Onset which was near at hand. But they
still behaved freindly until a large double canoe
came off from the shore. with several of the Principle
Inhabitance in her. This canoe was observed to hoist some
signal and the very instant all trade broke up, and in a few
secants of time our Decks was full of Great and small
stones, and several of our men cut and Bruisd. This
was so sudden and unexpected that we was some time
before we could find out the caus. We then found
Lenity would not do, therefor applyed to the Great Guns
and gave them a few round and Grape shot which struck
such terrors amongs the poor unhapy wretches that
it would require the pen of Milton's self to describe.

After all this orders was given that the Boats set out,
and in a few minutes Landed and formd on the Beach,
and with hoisting a Pennant took possession of the Island
In His Maj name, and Honourd it with the name
of our Most Gracious sovereign King George the third.

1 The Hearing

The case is Christian's mutiny. But your court
won't stomach that *Christian*. It smells of
mercy. This tale's awash like the *Bounty's*
bilge with meanings no one wants. We were all there, you
all saw, Adams, black Matthew, gunner Mills,
by Christ, Adam's mutiny! Jack Adams, John Doe,
every-man-Jack's mutiny! But your Lords
need a hanging, not this tale rippling
Irishly like a stone in a green lagoon.

I remember the white untidy beach, my head
a washed-up coconut jumping with sandflies.
If my fiddle were jailed and not fathom
five in the Barrier reef singing to catfish
I'd strike up a jig the court martial
would dance to! Michael Byrne, Irish fiddler,
two thirds blind, on trial for my life.

> *I kissed that maid and went away.*
> *Says she, young man, why don't ye stay?*

George Stewart, midshipman. That's a truly
life matter. Gentle George, drowned in leg-irons
in a panic of keys while your Captain Edwards

jumps ship as light and easy as he's danced
from your court. Tacks his ship on the coral?
Huzzah! Drowns his shipmates? Well away!
And George's bounty, sweet brown Peggy, who
ever chose a better wife in the South Seas
or England? Crouched on the poop by the cage
keening and I could smell the blood, George
heaving at his chains yelling she was bloodying
the baby and us cursing double Edwards
she was after carving open her scalp
with a shark's tooth.

> *All dark his hair, all dim his eye,*
> *I knew that he had said goodbye.*
> *I'll cut my breasts until they bleed.*
> *His form had gone in the green weed.*

Did she see her midshipman
dead in Edward's box on Great Barrier Reef?
A life matter truly! And now I recall
the oath he swore her in Matavai Bay
he'd never again set foot in muddy
England with its watery sun and broomsticks.
That sweet sundown with the wind offshore
drunk with blossoms no white man had named,
he held up his left arm to my better eye
and I squinted at a heart with a dart
through it and a black star. "What's this?"
I warbled, and he says "tattoo." Took him
all day and hurt like blazes. But permanent.
One of their words, tattoo. Strange how we
needed their lingo to make a landfall.

English boy, please tell to me
what is the custom in your country?

The new Cythera. Two volcanic breasts
and a fern-lined valley. Half a league
leeward you'd miss it. I'll say this for Bligh,
in the whole South Seas he'd smell out one
breadfruit tree on a rock. But Tahiti
scuttled us. There were oceans we couldn't
sail and that island named them: taboo.
Another locution we harboured. We're all
marked with Tahiti, hearts and stars
and commemorations. You, Millward, is it
God's truth you've Tahiti's chart on your yard
and compasses? Marrison, scratching your
journal of excuses, is your loving groin
gartered with *Honi soit qui mal y pense*?
How d'you hope to escape hanging after
pledges like that? Leave Bligh out of it,
truly the only blind man in Tahiti,
a pool fool with his rules and longitudes
while Michael Byrne, fiddler, kept watch.
Taboo: Christian's mutiny. Ten of us
Of twenty-five still waiting to be hung.

King Louis had a prison,
he called it his Bastille,
one day the people tore it down
and made King Louis kneel.

2 The First Man

Tahitohito,

>> the Fifth Age when
>> cunning gave birth to mockery.

>>>> First

was Ta'oroa the egg, tired of loneliness,
>> and his wife Stratum Rock,
Ta'oroa of sure bidding, of the cloudless sky,
>> who stood over the passage of the reefs.
Ta'oroa was a god's house, his backbone
>> the ridgepole, his ribs the buttresses.
Ta'oroa married his daughter Moon
>> and moulted red feathers from which grew
>> all plants except breadfruit tree.
Ta'oroa conjured Shark God and Rooster
>> and Octopus who clasped
>> earth to sky, smothering all light until
Ti'i stood forth, the first man,
>> and was angry,
Ti'i the boat-builder clothed in sand
>> was angry, demanding
light and he wrestled with Octopus' eight forearms
>> till sky floated free
>> shining with starlight and sunlight.
Then Ti'i the fire-maker, the axe-sharpener, was hungry
>> and his oven was sealed at daybreak
>> and opened at nightfall
>> but the meat was raw because
Sun was made drunk by space and hurtled like a meteor
>> until Maui his firstborn
roped his ten rays with ten anchor cables
>> and day became a task's length
>> and order was complete.

3 The Ship

Bounty, a word to sail in. We shipped it
south on a year's passage. Nine thousand
leagues, Bligh boasted, and I believe him.
For facts and cutlass words you'd trust Bligh.
But *Bounty* took his measure. God's humanity
in our navigation, our miraculous draught
of dolphins. In the larks which sang landfall.
In the albatrosses Bligh stuffed with corn
and baked like geese. That's *Bounty* reckoning
Bligh, God's munificence turned plunder. What
was our trade but packeting God's breadfruit
to the slavers? Bounty on a poacher's pelt,
or nigger's poll, or prize ship? Bounty
in the king's shilling? Bounty jumpers, Bligh
christened us, bountiful in his contempt.

> *Bounty was a grocer ship,*
> *pump ship, packet ship,*
> *cruising on a merchant trip*
> *in the South Pacific.*

So we shipped 'em a word to brawl over
while they screwed us raw for six-inch nails
they prised below deck from *Bounty*'s timbers.

Michael Byrne's *Bounty*? What's a sea trip
to a sightless man? The worst of my voyage
was Spithead, our salt baptism two dawns
afore Christ's birth. Such bullying winds
ambushed us as I never thought to be
pummelled by. Three days and nights of it, boats
stove in, cabins awash, beer casks overboard

for all we loitered like a Lime Street whore
with barely a stitch of canvass.

> *The Ol' Man shouts, the pumps stand by,*
> *oh, we can niver suck her dry,*
> *It's pump or drown the Ol' Man said*
> *or else damn soon ye'll all be dead.*

Cape Horn
likewise, the gales like a brick wall and seas
so criss-cross and contrariwise *Bounty*
jumps backwards like a march hare.

> *O round Cape Stiff in the month of May*
> *O round Cape Stiff is a bloody long way.*

For the rest
it was pay for a fiddler, and speaking
the truth as an Irishman I liked my perch
on the capstan sawing away, my rib cage
emptied of the ship's stink, sailing where reels
and hornpipes took me. On a blind voyage
you're corked in, like a ship in a green bottle.
I smuggled from the South Seas two score
ballads. Now my salt fiddle strikes 'em up
for George's bones jig-jigging in the coral.

153

4 The Kindest of Fathers

The Second Age was of trouble when nobles settled
                the high headlands
                and the gentry the quiet bays
and the commoners encroached everywhere, breaking
                down the bamboo fences of the great.
Then there came famine, so cloudless even the chiefs
                ate land crabs and red clay,
but Ruata'ata, kindest of fathers, led his wife and children
                to the mountains to gather ferns
and taking pity, his toes rooted and his fingers branched
                and he became Breadfruit tree
heavy with ripeness and his family feasted, and so trouble
                gave birth to wisdom.

5 The Ballad

Cape of Good Hope. Those old Portuguese
shipped their lingo with 'em, blessing the storms
with bread and wine. But a blind man harkens.
That Cape had its own rhythms. There's a point
we walked to, George Stewart and me, where oceans
touch. I never, not even in Ratcliffe Highway,
heard so many jawbreakers, Hollands, Malay,
Hindustani, a queer breed of nigger English.
Words club you in that town like the smell
of sweet natches and roast corn after quarters.

Africa's where I twigged Mr Christian.
It turned his head stomping feet on red soil
after the catwalk *Bounty*. He'd been chasing
butterflies under Table Mountain and caught

a ballad of a white woman and a babe
at a kraal, thirty days hence by the coastline.
That, and her song. She was always after
hugging the child. There wasn't a man-Jack
not pierced by this. What woman d'you see as I
tell you, Morrison?

> *Oh lady, have you a daughter fine*
> *for a sailor that's crossed the line?*

A song like that you
make up your own woman. Christian's was a child,
north country like himself, widow of the wreck
of an Indiaman. Pale cheeks, hair like tar.
That woman drowned all ours. If Bligh hadn't
cracked our heads where might we yet be grounded
with gentleman Christian? He'd words. That's
precipitous in a man that's done no living.

6 The Third Age

How hear of Helen the Budding Flower, her long hair
        sleek with sandalwood,
who so bewitched Tuiterai
        the womaniser, chief of Parara,
he sent shafts of feathers to her husband Tavi,
        chief of Tautira,
begging to possess her for seven days. "Seven nights
        only," he gave his oath,
and would return her in his war canoe with a gift
        of seven fat hogs.
Tavi for all his love was roped by courtesies
        to a fellow chief,

so Helen spent seven nights with Tuiterai the womaniser
                    and seven noons in his hut,
and he took the praise name Tuiterai Twin Breasts
                    so his courtiers sniggered.
But at the cold star of the eighth cockcrow,
                    Twin Breasts sang:

Why should I give up my treasure,
I, Tuiterai of the six skies?
Tie up the heavens like a net,
wrestle the clouds of Parara,
open the net and hang up to dry
the thousand knots that bind us.

Tavi heated his war drums and summoned his canoes
                    and laid Parara waste
carrying Helen home with necklaces of sharks' teeth on
                    each of the seven hogs,
while his warriors chased Tuiterai to the cloud base,
                    snaring him in a net, and were
wrestling him to the cliff's edge to hang up to dry
                    when Twin Breasts shouted
"No commoners may execute a chief
                    of the fortieth generation."
Tavi's warriors were silenced. Only Tavi
                    could kill Tuiterai.
Six days they carried him blindfold along the beaches
                    waiting for the warm tides,
and at each cold stream Twin Breasts dipped his hand
                    for he knew the touch of the waters.
The seventh cockcrow they brought him to Tavi's house
                    and Tavi despaired.
Between vengeance and courtesy there was no calm passage.
                    As his royal guest,

Tuiterai was securer than in his own compound, and lord
of his house and of Helen.

> *Take my wife, Twin Breasts,*
> *you have trapped her in your seine.*
> *I would die for her cloudless beauty,*
> *she is my morning and evening star.*
> *But take my dear wife, Tuterai,*
> *my heart strings are undone.*

7 South

The Pacific, wept by God in his blindness.
You'd steer twelve months on a half-wrong tack
and never hear breakers, the sun dangling so
high above the main mast even I squinted.
In the end the look-out was singing Ahoy
when birds appears, petrels and albatrosses.
They'd a trick of calling up a south wind
and at cockcrow we were among islands.

> *On the Bounty were the rules*
> *pump ship, packet ship,*
> *not for soft and silly fools*
> *in the South Pacific.*

This wasn't discovery. Cook knew 'em already
and that Frenchie they call Buggerville. From
Deptford Dock to the Spithead cathouses
we'd all whistled for the brown girls so
wet for sailors they'd do it on the beach
with their uncles watching. What we disputed,

Tom Birkett and me eight bells to four
by the lagoon where we supped on green mussels
and Muspratt swore the devil he was poisoned,
was AD 1773 carved on a trunk. A footprint
like Defoe's island. Where was that and whose
knife work was it? Our first landfall we were
tracking ourselves, imagining shipwreck.

>*Never was there heard a word*
>>*pump ship, packet ship,*
>*of the crew that stayed on board*
>>*in the South Pacific.*

8 The Handyman of Cunning

So wisdom was made foolish and Hiro flourished,
                handyman of cunning,
who sat astride the ridgepole of his grandfather's
                school learning
catches and chants and all poetry's riddles
                before he could walk.
What is a man's purpose? To build a house
                and get married.
What must I do with a wife? Feed her,
                and give her your cherishing.
That would be wasteful. Tell me what
                else men do?
Lying, thieving, raping, murdering. Good.
                Dishonesty
is profitable. It will be satisfying to a man.

9 Breadfruit

Nippled in your palm and heavy,
sweating like a green swamp.

> *I put my hand upon her thigh,*
> *Says she, Young man, ye're rather high.*

10 Tahitohito

So *Bounty* dropped anchor and we swaggered ashore
        girls draped on our necks
In the Fifth Age, *tahitohito*, when cunning
        gave birth to mockery.
They twigged at once we were the right gods
        for the times.
Our tricks with a foresail made 'em stare
        and our iron was like gold.
But nothing we did showed reverences, and we
        fucked anything that moved.
Then the ballads started. Cook's men were back,
        bleached like lepers,
Stinking like stale milk, our hides tattooed
        with brawling and the cat.
It confirmed the revolution and what better cockshy
        than Bligh himself
With his martinet's livery and his wooden wife
        in *Bounty's* figurehead?
We were *tahitohito*, the Fifth Age, and their worship
        was disbelief.

11 George

Landfall in Tahiti is hobbling barefoot
up a steaming path under the plantains,
a girl singing on your arm, steering you
to a ravine with a cliff like Wells Minster,
with ferns cold to the touch, and she says
"That's Tia-auru river", and you remember
the current surging from the cave, warm
with bats' dung, albino with catfish, so high
it took two days climbing into the clouds
and here, you can't believe it, falling as
rain. Staring up doesn't help. This is rain
and you're homesick, but Tia-auru has brimmed
Land's End in the sky and sheered to glass,
splintering to foam, dropping to nowhere,
a smoking slipstream, tugged by the breezes,
so light in its patter even the cloth-winged
butterflies flop through its mist, and you
perch on a flagstone, the girl on your arm,
her tar hair drenched by this river turned
to summer rain, and you stare at mutiny.

I'll cut my breasts until they bleed.
His form had gone in the green weed.

This was George Stewart's story. He'd been
up with his Peggy in the mountain farm
and the afternoon's descent was like shipwreck.
He gabbled of a pond with floating leaf-palettes
and a girl bathing tits-deep in the lilies.
Ho-hum, I says, where was Peggy? But he
was beyond gravelling, already marooned
by the green lagoon on the sickle beach,

Bounty's ribs charred on the headland.

> *Listening as I was not to her words*
> *but to the modulations of her voice*
> *and seeing as she gestured not the glades*
> *we walked in, only the poised grace*
> *of green light on her skin and she pointing,*
> *I can't now remember what we said*
> *or what she showed me, can't begin painting*
> *those leaves and vines, that sunlit river bed.*
> *But since her finger's pressure on my hand*
> *that day of mornings, nothing's as it was.*
> *Nothing seems alien now she understands.*
> *I deal no more in homesick ironies.*
> *This is my home, this still-discovering island*
> *ringed by such shores, such pelican-haunted seas.*

So George in love,
sonneteering. Next day they drummed his skin.
He held up his left arm to my better eye
and I squints at a heart and a black star.
"What's this?" and he tells me "Tattoo". Took
all day and hurt like blazes. But permanent.

12 Bligh

But how would old Bligh consider himself
politic? Show him seven skies of stars, he'll
prick 'em. But when he stalked the beaches
in full rig, sweating rank through his spine
and armpits, you'd hear *wei-wei, tahitohito,*
and hoots of belly laughter.

Who's the thief?
Tareu the thief
Stole Bligh's anchor-buoy.

                              Their women
got nowhere, not even Queen Purea who knew
she was better bred and made it statecraft
to service her. But this was another
Cook, besotted with his ship. Fingering
Bounty's timbers was stroking his woman.

I put my hand upon her hip,
Says she, Young man let's take a trip.

What crazed 'em were the iron good and muskets
he showered on mad chief Pomare – so much
it took a man-size sea chest to shut 'em in
with a padlock and clasp, Pomare's people
not troubling overmuch about ownership.
But Bligh's temper did the rest. When they saw
what tantrums they could wind him to over
tin pots or a thimble they'd him snared.
Before the end they were pocketing his crew.
They took George Stewart and Churchill, Millward
and Muspratt. They'd ways of thieving the heart
from your breastbone Bligh could never police.

October's moon they made their play. The *Arioi*
were in town, warrior actors with crimson
thighs and feather skirts driving the women
crazy with admiration. The *Arioi* could say
what they liked and take what they liked and we all
buzzed how they'd lampoon Bligh. It started
on the *Bounty* with Bligh feeding Pomare

like a nanny through seven courses of pork.
Upside down, you see, everything reversed.
Then we rowed 'em ashore and hoisted 'em
under the coconut arches to a clearing
with so many bonfires the *Arioi* called it
sun-copulating-with-moon. Aye, I was
there, with my bum at a fireside and a fistful
of ribs my fiddle had earned me, marvelling
how on that island I could always make out
candleflies, like scatters from the sunsets
that had me blinkered. But Bligh was an extra.
They kept him waiting, watching their play.
There were actors who weren't actors, *Arioi*
who weren't *Arioi* acting, and their argument
was theft. They sat feasting, keeping Bligh
in audience, till one of 'em would sneak his
neighbour's pork-knuckle, and they bounced up
and danced in a line:

> *Who's a thief?*
> *Tarue the thief*
> *Stole Bligh's rudder.*

                    So they turned Bligh
overseer, and perched at their feast again,
till someone colonised a breadfruit slice:

> *Who's a thief?*
> *Tarue the thief*
> *Stole Bligh's compass.*

Then they changed their burlesque, from Bligh
without bearings to Bligh the woman-hater.
By Christ, I loved it. They're blinder to books

than Michael Byrne but they read their enemy.
Bligh shouldered the baskets and bolts of calico
and the suckling pig he'd been told to bring 'em
back and forth from the cutter like poor Jack Tar
to the Big Men staring down from the platform.
There were nine of 'em, lounging on their stools,
twirling their toes and languid fly-whisks, frowning
like judges at a fart till one of 'em sang out:

> *I am the comedian of this land*
> *That vibrates with the gun.*

He uncurled, all seven foot of him, strutting
like a bird of paradise and taunted Bligh,
husband of the *Bounty*, hater of thieves,
whether he'd children in his own country. So
there was Bligh, untouched by woman, confessing
to fatherhood and, by God, they made him lumber
back to the cutter for a second forfeit.
This time they'd a speech for him. Pomare
Cued him line by line and he thought 'twas his
accent convulsed while the *Arioi* sat deadpan:

> *This is the age without meaning,*
> *No payment, just copulation,*
> *Copulation to climax, one after another.*
> *The mouth does not even have to call out,*
> *The eyes say all that is necessary*
> *Until we have made our circle of Tahiti*
> *Copulating, copulating, copulating.*

Bligh stood there cunning in his livery
with the crowd whoop-whooping at every line,
but he couldn't see ourselves in their mirror.

The man thought he was diplomatising, getting
Bounty pregnant with breadfruit on the cheap.

13 Christian

Study, he said, *this land without King George*
To keep raw anger rising in your gorge,
Without a throne, an altar or Bastille
To crush the people with an iron heel,
This soil where natural man's impulses flow
Along the channels mapped by Jacques Rousseau,
Unlike the land we sailed from with such pains
Where man born free is everywhere in chains.
Who would not choose to live where Nature proffers
Shelter and dress and food from ample coffers,
Where artificial needs are yet unstudied,
The Horn of Plenty generous and unbloodied.
Who would not choose to die ...

                    So the rocking horse
of his class. It took Christian to mutiny
in couplets. I told him his French hero was
mad George's pensioner. But Tahiti scarred him
less than Bligh. Nature. Simplicity. Every
word he uttered was heavy with England.
If he'd stayed home he'd have seen his Liberty
and the Bastille burning. Now he's cruising
the South Seas with his skull full of words.

14 Possession

"Boys dream," says our native poet, "of native
girls bringing breadfruit – whatever they may be.

> *I put my hand upon her cunt.*
> *Says she, Young man, take what ye want.*

15 Mutiny

Perfumed Oil's hair was a ballad sung
              by the summer wind to a calm ocean
and four brothers harkened and set sail in a canoe
              with four thatched cabins,
but when they anchored off the island
              of Perfumed Oil's inheritance, she was
away in the woods collecting sweet smelling ferns
              for the arrival she had foretold,
and her servant girl welcomed the brothers, hiding
              the stench of her ordinariness
with scented oils from her mistress's gourds, so three
              brothers were deceived,
carrying the maid to the canoe where the youngest
              brother kept watch.
Perfumed Oil returned and found her gourds
              and girdle of feathers
stolen, so she embarked on her surfboard, swimming
              a day and a night
and accosted the eldest brother, "Take me
              up into your vessel,"
and the second brother the same, and the third
              until the youngest
took pity, offering her pork ribs and fresh water

and the safety of his cabin.
But the canoe was becalmed and the air grew foul
                and the servant girl shouted
"See how the imposter has stolen the fresh breeze
                along with my sweet odour,"
and three brothers were deceived, casting Perfumed Oil
                into the whirlpool
where Shark God received her in his cavernous mouth
                and sank to his lair.
The sisters in Papeete were preparing to receive a bride
                but the feather banners
refused to stand upright and the perfume gourds
                split open, and when
the maid was carried ashore on the tallest man's
                shoulders, she could
not alight on the mats where the sisters walked freely
                but cowered in the latrine.
So the truth tumbled out and the youngest brother sailed
                back to the whirlpool,
pouring oil on the waves and chanting his poems
                till Shark God delivered
shipshape and Bristol fashion the wife
                of his pity and desire.

Not a strong tale to my Irish mind, needing
ballast from a tune with a deep undercurrent
though the stench of my ordinariness maybe
fogs the finer points. But here's anchorage.
This ballad Christian whistled and begged me
to master and my drowned fiddle humoured him.
For all his mutinies he liked this tale
of the younger, sea-going brother like himself
scooping the princess and the inheritance.
I sang it from the capstan not two hours

afore Bligh's lilibolaro about his missing
coconuts – aye, the *Arioi* knew about that too.
We were likely Tahitians in winding Bligh
to bedlam over his Christian property.
That night, Christian looked to jump the taffrail
with a surf board and Shark God came for him,
circling the *Bounty* with one fin showing,
signalling love from the moon's track in the water.
That's the tale the *Arioi* wove in their dancing,
Christian called back to the island by the god.
But he disobeyed and took the *Bounty* instead
so we're all to stretch necks, the gods not
winnowing impulses like your English court.

Christian had no bride, just a Catherine
or two in Papeete. It was gentle George
and brown Peggy had a tale of their own.
But Shark did come. He fired your mutiny
in a clamour for muskets to take pot shots
at death. What happened next was sorcery,
a pother of fulminations and not a shipmate
bruised. I was dangling like a hanged man
in the cutter and heard all your contrariness
and the cowardice of those they're calling heroes.
The *Arioi* followed their sense of what fits.
Three years on you've nothing so well shaped.

16 The Question

So what was your *Bounty* cellmates? Not a man
of you nobly mutinous. Did you collar
Bligh in his nightshirt? Then why
Portsmouth, Tom Birkett? It's no harbour
for that history. And Elly, lad, Tom Ellison,
"I'll be sentry over him", will ye? The last
of the *Bounty* Bligh saw was your arse aloft
losing the top gallant. You're a child, Tom,
no pirate. And you're his twin, Heywood. No
pleading family here. That cutlass. Why did
your hand touch it? Did you know that daybreak?
D'you know three summers on? Yet you hallooed
Edwards, come to hang you, like a schoolmate.

> *The fiddler took up his fiddle*
> *and merrily he did play*
> *the Scottish jig and hornpipe*
> *and then the Irish hey.*

Muspratt likewise. A carcase tanned like yours
should know its mind. I heard the cat, twelve
lashes, then two dozen and twenty-four more.
Bligh says you're much marked and he should know.
And you, Millward, who never picked your nose
but Churchill ordered you. Or Morrison scribbling
your journal of exculpation. Why aren't you
sailing the South Seas in Christian's *Bounty*?
Coleman might cheat the rope, and McIntosh
And Norman. Bligh promised he'd see you right.
The rest of you'll hang for contrariness.

17 Oro

Even the gods hadn't foreseen this Sixth Age
                of Horrors
when breadfruit tree's shadow, shook by Ta'oroa,
                moved across Hina-the-Earthbound
and she grinned up at the shade which instructed her
                "Here are Ta'aroa's genitals,
stand and examine them and insert them."
                So Oro was born.
                Oro the rabid pig
one jaw pointing to the sky, the other
                to the red earth, gaping
for "man-long-bananas" on his altar of skulls,
                Oro the sixth finger,
bandaged bloodily, on the left hand
                of Tahiti the fish.

18 The Action

After your mutiny 'twas a different island.
It made fresh fools of all of us except
George and sweet Peggy. I danced to Papara,
crazy about the *Arioi* and women, keeping
downwind of your battles. Old Purea
liked my fiddle, and I'd as sound a perch
on a canoe in her courtyard as on *Bounty's*
capstan. I never knew they'd coined Oro
in our mould. When you'd your way, Morrison,
and made that dunce Pomare king, the eyes
gouged from the sacrifices plucked even
mine open. Christian's *noblesse oblige*

made 'em noble savages. Now they were
primitives and we'd guns.

> *Mit mein niggerum, buggerum, stinkim,*
> *Mit mein niggerum, buggerum, stinkim,*
> *Vell, ve'll climb upon der steeples*
> *And ve'll shit down on der peoples.*

                        You want me to sing
of your wars, Morrison? I can track you
in my twilight, scratching at your book
of righteousness. I know what you're thinking
to flatter your Lords with. The poor natives
needed government, did they? You'd found out
they were tribesmen and tribes are hooligans
in the wise reign of our George. That island
glowed with its bellbirds and candleflies and the sea
in the casuarinas and the courtyards you'd
dawdle into and squat on a stump and with
two bars of "Willow, willow" have everyone
quiet as breathing. For you, 'twas for sieges,
stratagems, night marches and ambuscades,
your stinking groin gartered with *Honi soit*,
and for what blunt end? To make Pomare
king with his wits as addled as our George's!
That's princely flattery, Morrison. That'll
buy you reprieve.

> *Tweedle-Dee*
> *And Tweedle-Dum*
> *Bow your head*
> *And raise your bum.*

171

So Tahiti's tribes came
against you like they'd never hated Bligh,
pitching down the mountainsides from the nor-west
and west and all points of the compass south
in a real mutiny, one that knew its business.
Only your guns succoured you while Pomare
clapped his ears against the bang bang of murder.

Don't boast you'd no hand in it. I heard you
at Parara when Pomare despatched
his coronation standard and people smothered
their cooking fires and hid in the forest. You
saw for all its feathers, 'twas the Union jack
and barked fusillades in King George's honour.
English colours, English powder.

> *Pop-pop went the muskets,*
> *Bang went the gun,*
> *Crash went the cannon*
> *And out went the sun.*

Those last days
on Tahiti, we all traipsed like schoolboys
to the temple Pomare had built for Oro,
the war god your taboos bestowed on him.
All your tribes submitted. Only Vehiatua's
people raised their skirts and bared their arses
at your flag. The rest looked to the mountains
when their children were speared through the right
ear and dragged behind canoes to Pare
and flung before the new king of Tahiti
who sat with his mouth open while the priests
skewered their eyeballs with bamboo splints.
Aye, it's true,

172

Pandora saved you, Morrison. Double Edwards,
of all captains, arrested you in your frenzy.

19 Shipwreck

Night on Great Barrier Reef and white seas,
Edwards laying to, panicking at fifty
fathoms, putting about, grounding broadside,
eleven hours foundering and every Jack-in-office
jumps ship while thirty-one able shipmates
drown. It should have sunk him. Yet he swans
from your English court oblivious of shallows.

> *A bully ship with a bully crew,*
> *But the captain's a bastard through and through.*

I remember breakers pitching coconuts like
cannonfire. Then the scalding beach razored
with coral. Shipwreck for George who willed it
by a pond with blue lilies and afterwards Peggy
carving her scalp with a shark's tooth. Does she
weep he's betrayed her, gone so long? We beached
in our skins, thumping like catfish, and George
was drowned, and Hanover Henry with his old
satire our mad king was his uncle's uncle.
Scarface John was dead and young Dick Skinner.

> *'An if we drown while we are young,*
> *better to drown than wait to be hung.*

So jail's present tense, a restful anchorage.
There'll be no burning Bastilles here, only

a long war with us Irish the likely losers.
Your lords have a style of using islands
as cudgels in a war with yourselves. If 'twas
freedom you sought, Tom Ellison, Tom Birkett,
you should've drifted with your chance. Somewhere
in the South Seas Christian and Jack Adams,
Black Matthew and Martin and gunner Mills
have burned their *Bounty* and settled their wars.
We homed in irons and found Bligh bobbing
and beribboned after a thousand leagues
fine seamanship, every man-Jack saved
with the salt water inches from his gunnels.

Strange, I could make out candleflies. Show
Bligh seven skies of starts he'll prick 'em, blind
to the bounty dazzling this sightless man.

20 Sentence

We took our quarrels with us
and dark imaginings,
we found a laughing people,
we left behind a king.

> *English boy, please tell to me*
> *what is the custom in your country?*

Michael took up his fiddle
and mournfully did play
the Scottish pibroch
and the Irish well-away.

Where are the men who seized the ship
and sailed into the dawn?
Where are the men who dangled?
They hang tomorrow morn.

My love weeps in the South Seas
dark by a calm lagoon
where coconut flags are silver
in the torchlight of the moon.

Where are the men who seized the ship
and sailed into the night?
My babe's head is bloodied,
my salt-sea bones are white.

Louis was the King of France
before the Revolution.
Today they cut his turnip off
and spoiled his constitution.

Michael took up his fiddle
and merrily did play
the Scottish jig and hornpipe
and then the Irish hey.

> *Sweet George, please tell to me*
> *what is the custom in your country?*

Postscript: Landfall

HMS Beagle: 1835

October 20: At first light, Tahiti
was in view. As soon as we anchored
in Matavai Bay, we were ringed by canoes.
This was our Sunday, but the Monday
of Tahiti: if the case had been reversed,
we should not have received a single
visit; for the injunction not to launch
a Sabbath canoe is strictly obeyed.

> *She wears red feathers*
> *And a hoola hoola skirt,*
> *She wears red feathers*
> *And a hoola hoola skirt.*
> *She lives on*
> *Just coconuts*
> *And fish from the sea,*
> *A rose in her hair*
> *A gleam in her eye*
> *And a love in her heart for me.*

Everyone brought conch shells for sale.
Tahitians now understand money and much
prefer it to parrot feathers or nails.
The various coins, however, of English
and Spanish denomination puzzle them;
they never seem to think the small silver
quite secure until changed into dollars.

> *I work in a London bank*
> *Respectable position,*

From nine to three
They serve you tea
But ruin your disposition.
Each night at the music hall
Travelogues I'd see
And once a pearl
Of a native girl
Came smiling right at me.

There are many who scorn the missionaries'
improvements and dub Presbyterian the ban
on night revelry and the nose flute.
Such reasoners never compare the present
island with that of twenty years ago. They
forget, or will not remember, that human
sacrifices, an idolatrous priesthood,
profligacy unparalleled, bloody wars – all
these have been abolished: and dishonesty,
intemperance and licentiousness reduced.

Tired of the London bank
I started out a sailing.
Fourteenth day
From Mandalay
I spied her from the railing.
She knew I was on the way
Waiting, and was true.
She said, you son
Of an Englishman,
I dreamed last night of you.

Queen Pomare was persuaded to dine
on the Beagle. Four boats were sent
and the yards manned on her Majesty's

coming on board. The Tahitians behaved
most properly. They begged for nothing
and seemed content with their presents.
The queen is a large, graceless woman
with only one Royal attribute: a perfect
immovability of expression under all
circumstances, and that a rather sullen one.
Rockets were fired. After each explosion
a deep "ah" echoed from all points
of the moonlit bay. Our sailors' shanties were
much admired. Of one, the Queen declared
"It most certainly could not be a hymn".

> *I'm back here in London town*
> *And though it may seem silly,*
> *She's with me*
> *And you should see*
> *Us stroll down Piccadilly.*
> *The boys at the London bank*
> *I know they hold their breath.*
> *She sits with me*
> *And drinks her tea*
> *Which tickles them to death.*

Unwittingly, I was the means of my companions
breaking their own laws. I had with me
a flask of spirits, which they could not
refuse to partake of: but as often as they
drank they put their fingers before their
mouths, and uttered the world "Missionary".

5

Purchase

So I come again to design a garden
with more space than I know how to fill.
Poetry, even the translated epic's no
match for the puppy from the next allotment's
outrage at my furrow-skipping shoes.
I scratch his ears and pronounce *Bom dia*
to its quizzical owner and barrel-shaped wife.
"Are you coming to live?" I tell them, *sim*.
"To plant vegetables?" "Fruits". They gesture
to their grove of golden citrus. "Your place
is full of rabbits". And so we begin.
                          An acre,
more or – "Less", contends Alice (whose
husband-less grandmother hoed each rains
four hectares, living by such husbandry).
Back at the *armazem*, she protests
at my raincoat. "There was a puppy,"
                          I explain.
Armazem, or *barracão*, cobwebbed roof,
serviceable walls. A fortnight after we've
bought it, the agent locates the keys.
We descend into a gloom of bat-droppings,
barrels, two hundred bottles, a wine-press
a pruning hook, a torch by way of w.c.
The pan-tiles are a starlit sky. I make
swipes with a rusty sickle. But candles,
a good spot to see out the millennium. His
bunk, whoever he was, is here. His mirror
                          reflects me.

My Latest Journey

My latest journey to the city
takes 50 minutes and 100 years.
I start out across a field, and wait
at the bus stop by the junction store
with women travelling to market
and old men going nowhere,

and we descend, even in August,
into a greenery so profound
the plunge annihilates all thought
this ride could have an end,
till the old men raise their hats
at the cemetery to their friends,

then each delay us, negotiating
the coach's narrow exit,
separately manipulating
hip, knee or humped back
the members that adumbrate
they're still among the quick.

The women take their elbows
clucking with motherly concern,
rewarded by a formal bow
from each gallant in his turn.
The automatic door hisses
behind them on its piston.

Then it's the *via rapida*,
the half full bus half my age,
and the emblematic barrier
of a stony mountain ridge

between here and the city where
we pretend to a monthly wage.

The girls look like sisters
with delicate cheek bones,
and high-waisted trousers
with enigmatic chains;
like auto-palm readers
they study their mobile phones.

The men are less disguisable,
more obviously their fathers'
sons in suits, more individual,
tolerant of the stranger
absorbed in his foreign journal,
and unimpressed by rumour.

I stare down from the motorway
at what we've left behind,
villages deep in the twisting valley,
anciently confined,
shaped by the land's fertility,
not by a turn of mind,

for there's nothing up here, not
even a windmill, just scrub
and abandoned quarries. Hermit
territory once perhaps,
or a *basse terre* for bandits,
but I can make out ships

in the estuary, and the towers
of the city's suspension
bridge. Consumers

loom, with a quickening
of interest, as the bus
tilts and the new horizon's

a jagged ring of apartment
blocks patrolling the moors,
forbidding as ancient
megaliths, or survivors
of a nuclear blast, painted
as we descend closer

pink and turquoise and curry
yellows, no flowering
in balconies or weathered
stone for those here
to rise up in the world,
entombed on the 10th floor.

For the heart of the city's
on, beyond the jammed
viaduct, the ring road supermarkets,
beyond the latest stadium,
where something's played out,
older than the millennium,

younger than the last CD shop
perched, sublimely ignorant,
on the ultimate outcrop
of this many-layered settlement.
Appropriately, we stop,
where the metro first descends,

tunnelling through history
to our individual stations,

my fellow villagers and I,
through pre-Roman foundations,
Visigothic debris,
Moorish irrigations,

the Crusaders' rubble,
the Navigators' bricolage,
the earthquake's upheaval,
all that to emerge
at this pre-industrial level
of a post-industrial age,

for the city's trend's
linear, with arrival
endlessly postponed.
First person plural,
this journey's end's
a recurring trick of style.

The Brown Girl

When on the molasses barge, reading Austen's
Orgulho e Preconceito, she was even then,
in the swamplands, plotting houses on envelopes,

Reader, we begin this poem a long way
back, with the brown girl, just twenty-one,
on a flooded tributary of the green Zambesi,

sketching rooms for family, for sleeping
and cooking, and a hatchet-hewn
fig wood table, seating not less than twenty,

steaming upriver, the reed plumes
whitening at dawn. Motionless, the current
slides, duckweed debris spinning

in a long room with a ceiling fan and wooden
shutters, a veranda with anthuriums
in milk tins, a treadle Singer humming,

in the black eddies. The river coils
back on itself. A hippo surfaces,
yawning like a piano. Acres of lilies undulate

at the head of a flamingo estuary,
with some land like her mother's rice farm
somewhere. Thirty years on her loveliness

as the barge blunders on sunrise, a dugout
on the gold inlet, a net swirls and is cast,
while over their water pots, braless women

no longer blank, she is flawed with beauty.
Such things are hardly to be written of
– like the offering of beer and maize flour,

semaphore to the bargemen their satiric
invitations, as she turns the page, prettily
incensed by Darcy's too proud proposal.

the pumpkin leaves with coconut, she
pledges in this foreign corner, hallowing
in her mother's name, this plot before she builds.

Casa Uhuru

Flywell Ntima of that forgotten generation
for whom Pan Africanism would redeem
the world, has brought his wound
to a small estate, here in the Alentejo,

and stubbornly named it *Casa Uhuru*.
We have much in common, he and I, though
the same history scuppered my chances
of being a kindly DC on perpetual safari,

or a folklore crazed missionary. Our journeys
have brought us to plots in Portugal
in a pretence of putting down roots where race
is not too much of an issue. Our difference

lies in his greater ambition – viz., the flecked
bamboo he smuggled from the Ivory Coast
and watches like a nurse, or the evening
his French wife phoned him in Nairobi

to say the fever tree was in fresh shoot, and he
spent the whole night tossing in excitement.
As for his baobabs, he has three in pots,
stunted like bonsai, but in tiny leaf.

Imagine a savannah trembling with thorn trees,
a black mountain, cut by a highway,
where the poor have access and the educated prosper.
His *Casa Uhuru*'s a dream this dreamer's lost.

Arab Work

Alice is designing a water garden
at the foot of the slope in the swamp
under the plum tree, with Easter
lilies and six types of melon. But,
it turns on a blocked waterway,
easily reverted to its proper course
– too late, though, for the plum
that in its death throes hurls
me as I climb to prune it.

Now the land's harrowed, I
recognise for the first time
what I've unseen five times:
the stone trough, the square
stone culvert, smooth as an egg,
tunneling our plot to the arched
exit. This is Arab work, a well-
watered platform raised a thousand
years back at the valley's head,

and my unfolding luck's to have
purchase where the husbandry
of a millennium still holds.
The olive trees are archives,
the soil clinging to my shoes
has been turned so many centuries
by tools that have kept their
shape and muscle. My sudden
prayer is serious: to be worthy.

Melting-Pot

The delights of a mixed-marriage! She
hoists a hoe, I heel a spade, but here's

no word for calling a spade a spade.
I decline the shoulderless tin shovel

they proffer me, ("um pā", they call it.
"Umpa, umpa," I practice, humming Elgar's

Cockaigne), and to buy what's what
must descend to the Princess Di Emporium

declaring, whenever I plant a tree
(round peg, admirably square hole),

I'm a bife from above the hoe-line,
beyond the olive and cork oak line

where wives are frigid and cuisine
never penetrates, where we drink

warm beer at silly-mid-on, and bury
our dead in churchyards, and where

(spades being trumped) *my*
deadliest insult founders: to my

"You Bastard!" your *under-the-belt*
body blow hisses "Cuckold!"

– though being as I am snow-bound,
embracing the dusky south,

how then explain she lusts for
not you, my pork-and-cheese *senhor*,

but tea on a Tennysonian
lawn barricaded with roses?

Before the Oranges have Fallen

Bonfire, good fire (Johnson, 1755),
not hell's torment, nor the Inquisition's
auto-da-fé, nor England's yearly

carbonisation of Guy, but benign,
necessary flames. Prune, and burn
before planting, ash for the soil

and pleasure for the soul. On a crisp
afternoon, with an Atlantic view,
and a robin inspecting sawn-off

lichens, as my smoke's shadow
purples the up-turned earth,
I am feeding a fire, with plum

and apple prunings. This
isn't Tyger, nor Hopkins' forge,
nor Eliot's dove with the flickering

tongue descending in damnation,
nor am I priest nor presbyter
consummating the millennium, just

a man greying with average wisdom,

glad that spring comes early here
before the oranges have fallen,

ignorant of any need to make
poetry of the fact I love
lighting and tending a bon fire.

Revisiting Grasmere

There was a time the English read Wordsworth
with delight and instruction, plummeting
depths in themselves and patterns
in their understanding
of work and time and love given,
but who reads poetry now,
or can pronounce
from the century just past
two hundred lines by heart?
Our most intimate art
mislaid its audience.

There's a sort of finch settles
late afternoon on the telephone wire
a dozen feet from my veranda
and blasts away at me, shrill
as an Irish fiddle and as tuneless:
what he's about I've no idea.
Or the woodpecker
with the scarlet poll,
drilling away at the creosote pole
as though it were still a tree,
what are his Black and Decker
lobotomies to me?

Line breaks, for example,
that elementary mark of verse,
visible at twenty paces
whatever the language or competence,
how did the lack of imagination's pressure
for the turn to occur at just
that point
come, like the absence of rhyme,
to be called reform?

Today, raking mown
meadow flowers for the autumn
bonfire, I frightened a tiny
wriggling snake and close by
a baby weasel. Does
our plot connect them?
The snake slid like a boot lace
down a crack in the summer
crust. The needle-toothed
perfection I cremated.

The *canna* burns with rifle shots
and little diapason sighs;
the ivy flares like linoleum.

Yet in any airport or shopping mall, any coach
or hotel or motorway toilet, even on beaches and our
voyage to the source of the Golden River,
the young's crude quatrains
boom

   Boom,
   Let's go back to my room,
   We can do it all night,
   Make me feel all right –

they're classics,
    idols, legends to their face, their self-
    belief baffles irony, their rhymes
    are in deepest space, brute instinct
    in tune with the void.

These swallows milling like termites
in the indigo glow of dusk
scream too, clicking
in their African dialects.
What makes me, so out of touch
with the times, feel
there's knowledge there, if only
I could glean it? They have
come so far, they're so
excellent at what they do,
scudding and scything
with such thrilling grace
as though meaning were not an issue.

To create the taste
you would be judged by,
to mirror the complexity of the times,
to bring all life within compass,
to discipline emotion's squadrons,
words strictly at attention,
to create the exact, unsullied
image, to shock, expose,
bewilder, fool,
look in thy heart and write,
fool, look in your heart,
the foul second-hand shop, where
boom-boom the poem starts.

These storm clouds, scudding across
the night sky over the heaving
Atlantic, are not so black
as the one pine tree
silhouetted where our garden drops.
Night, but I can find my way
to its chequered bark
blindfold. After day's particulars,
night reminds us how we hang in space,
squandering our inheritance,
more than ever dependent
on its necessary companion
art – to cut the diamond metaphor,
ridicule all courtiers, burnish
the other in ourselves, praising
the guerrilla warfare of flowers.

In this late October gale
the sickle moon is intermittent:
anchored planets and hurtling stars
gleam, and go out, and radiate again.

Mightier than, etc.

For Senhor João Fonseca Gil Vincent,
his bulldozer's a precision instrument.

He could smash that 200 year olive bole
with a single uppercut, and does the inevitable,

but he prefers a featherlite dusting, a neat
filleting of culverts and driveways, that

depends on exact poise, viz., four
pile-driving telescopes opening at singular

angles to calibrated levels
(the millstone tyres revolving

uselessly) so the contraption rears
like a monster cockroach, and our senhor

with his gap-toothed digger
and a battery of levers

pats and smooths and nudges and prods
his boulders and clods

as though icing a cake,
or planting a mosaic,

or crafting a more elegant lyric
than these elephant-foot iambics,

– for as he watches the writer
watching the constructor

there's detectable irony
in his reined-in delicacy.

The mightier pen,
the sword into ploughshare,

hardly seem options
when it's ballpoint and bulldozer.

A Thing about Wrens

A thing not widely known about wrens
is that the male, before February's done,

builds three or four different nests to display
like an estate-agent to prospective Jennies

and if one clicks, he gets off with her.
This explains the behaviour

we've been jointly ogling
like gossips through the bedroom curtain,

viz., why there was no conjugal action for so long
beyond the glorious reveille of that song.

We guess she dropped by: *I like the garden,*
complimenting our birthday jasmine,

but the interior needs fixing, which
is why he flew in with the extra lichen,

and sang more fiercely, and this time scored.
As for the nests not owner-occupied,

those tiny balls, domestic
as tea cosies, intricate

as an Arraiolos weave,
virtual houses, never

to be hatched in, in the bramble
perhaps, or the cork oak or laurel,

poems perfected
but never read,

does he revisit them, imagining other lives
he might have invented with different wives?

Old Sonnet

We stop at Adão, the smith's workshop.
Our arches shine in the gloom, awaiting
only a protective coat, and so shaped
and proportioned I seriously debate
abandoning our purple tunnel of grapes
and allowing his wrought-iron art
to soar and descend on its own terms. As I grip
his oily, metallic palm, he repeats
what I can deduce for myself, the trope
of stress and strain as opposites.
Each is precisely what I'd dared to hope,
as strict and radiant as an old sonnet,
and, of course, vines must do their duty,
completing purpose, re-doubling beauty.

Trees

1
Cork oak, native to the Alentejo, a sort of
Irish-joke tree, yielding by way of pillage
not nuts nor sugar, but its very bark

in a below-the-waist striptease – an affair

of double negatives, as Lisbon humour has it.
You see them half-naked, their blacks

or mahogany bold as paintwork, each rising
from the pool of its own shadow
on the dry plain rolling to the Spanish border.

Southey, not the most nimble of poets,
thought cork oaks the loveliest trees of all.
Unfarmed, on the slopes of Sintra mounain

or in the natural forest of Monchique,
they turn pure gothic, harbouring creepers,
orchids, bats, and old lichens in fantastic

silhouettes, their masks furrowed as old
Auden's. A poet's tree, then, faintly
absurd, and most so when commercial,

– like the Alentejo peasants who
crop but don't own them, so
married to their hats they won't

enter a church, and anciently without
substitute for sealing the distillation of each
autumn on autumn's vintage.

2
Bluegums (*Eucalypti Globali*) aren't
liked here. They leach the soil,
bequeathing dustbowls. They're

commercial, compounding profit

in a mere ten years, something no
self-respecting tree should do. They uphold

concrete on ten thousand building sites,
Globalus being, like the builders themselves,
immigrant. Yet you'd never know

from its on-camera speed of growth
how tough this wood is. Creosoted,
it'll choke your drill, and a two-handed

frame-saw's needed to bring one to logs.
A graceful tree, tall as a poplar,
slender as a birch, its foliage

silver fish in a noon of August heat.
At the marginale turn-off,
an ancient ex-pat, a century young,

can be scented at 50 metres,
twice that after rain, its camphor
easing the fevers of the whole *bairro*.

3

Vine root's a twenty foot black
mamba fossilised in its writhing,

its knots untieable, its grip defying
earth-movers – for which

the two hundred year olive bole's
a mere ninety seconds yank. Across

bulldozed vineyards, they shoot
lime-fresh each April

as if the mechanical dinosaur
were an elaborate pruning hook.

Nothing we take in draws on deeper
arteries than grape vines, yielding

Ogun, Christ, and Dionysius,
so the most charitable,

murderous, inspired drunk's
in league with something of himself.

4
Then there's the religious orthodoxies
of the olive oil presses, viz.,

"ten per cent virgin", or better
"seven per cent extra", that

first odourless ooze without a menstrual trace of green
(but how can three per cent be purer than the ten?

degrees of virginity
more baffling than the Trinity).

I love the taste of olives
with their maculate, Arab flavour

and I like the stubbornness of olive trees,
the light that flashes from their metal leaves

like the mercury fountain in the Alhambra,
or the Cordoba

mosque with its bright logic
– viz., the most sacred relic

in old Glastonbury was a section
of the hole in which Christ's

tree stood. Holy, holey,
wholly, Lord God Almighty,

"gaze on this reliquary,
which is only apparently empty"

(and had they ninety-per-cent
or the infinitely purer ten?)

St Thomas with your loving doubt,
among the disciples, you were the poet!

Water

This long summer with the oily tips.
of lemon trees curling like copper shavings,
I'm getting to know our *poço*

well. As the valley turns sepia,
and olive trees sharpen their knives,
and the blue gums are shoals of silver fish,

I draw on its quick secrets. At noon,

the shutter thrown back, sunlight
arrows down the green whitewash

to a shimmering, infinitely
beckoning circle and beyond
to water snake flashes in an abyss

impossible to climb from.
Subsisting attuned to a well,
watching the trees breath, drinking

in bird song's a throwback
to develop, so
picture me, with my native off-spin,

bowling a plastic bucket to shatter
my face framed in the mirrored
hatch and haul miracle

draughts earth-wards, well
aware if it doesn't flow,
I'm not working hard enough.

Literary Remains

Vasco's used to the latest custom,
but his father was appalled when
between the lying-in and the burial
the corpse was abandoned overnight.

"Overnight? In England, it's frozen
in the morgue till the family

drifts in from wherever with time
off work, maybe ten days or more."

Now it's Vasco's scandalised. But he
has a grim duty. Here, the buried enjoy
a five year tenure before the bones
are lifted and boxed in the vault,

this resurrection needing a family
member present in law to approve
– his aunt, for instance, so embalmed
by her pills she took seven years

to qualify for the skeleton cupboard.
Babies, says Vasco, disturb him most
with their tiny rosaries and bird-like
ribs, and I yield him the palm

in this tournament of the macabre,
he being half my age in a matter ever
closer to the bone, and I far from re-
hearsed in my curtain-line rattle.

Roman Style

The scythe's discarded blade with its gap tooth
rusts on the veranda. Spring's flowers
are levelled, the field's pared

to contours the swallows shave unerringly.
Our feeling's of summer no sooner come
than gone, but l never cease marvelling

about the seasons here, how harvest's
but a prelude to Julho and Agosto,
Roman inserted months, when the sun

scours like a blow torch, and our resort's
once more to our well-spring. It's not
what we are at heart feels different,

perhaps a little heavier, somewhat
slower to the beach ball, while judges,
presidents, even golfers, are ever younger,

and no TV adverts target us in their mooning
mock-Hollywood, thank god, for jeans
or face creams or exercise contraptions

as friends are crossing into the dark,
and it touches family ever closer. So,
the hatch sealed, we've sized up the well

with a pump buoy, and regale nightly
all we've planted with more than ever
loving and lavish draughts, hoping

Roman-fashion to insure against
something when the scythe rounds
on its owner and the plot lies bare.

A Different Valley
(after Virgil's 1st Eclogue)

Luís

Taliesin (what kind of name's that?), I watch you scribbling
there on your veranda with your sandals on that tiled table
glorying in your grapes and peppers, your apples and walnuts,
while I'm being evicted from this fertile valley I've
known every inch of since before I learned my catechism.
I'm expelled from my fields with my goats and my ancient wife
to put up with my daughter in the next town, while you loll
in leafy shade, pretending to pretend your trees and flowers
come together in praising your "beautiful Carapinha".

Taliesin

Luís, it's Welsh, and I've a patron, a young fogy in a suit
who likes to practise his English. So long as I make him
monthly offerings, he gives me ample freedom to compose.

Luís

I don't grudge any man his freedom, but I have to tell you
this could never have happened under the dictatorship! I
should
have checked my *Borda d'Agua* when that lightening bolt
struck the cork oak in my yard. Look, my pet she-goat
can hardly move. She dropped her twins on builders' rubble
in the shadow of a concrete wall, where I remember olive trees
and a perennial stream. Now my landlord wants my cottage
and allotment to re-develop as a petrol station. But tell me
about this lord of yours. Who is he with all his largesse?

Taliesin

That city you call Lisboa, there on the Tagus – in my folly
I thought it a city of squares and funiculars and pavement

cafes, a quiet retreat from empire, where the best food by far
is by far the cheapest. Yet these days with the euro, I kid
you not, Lisbon's a great place for every kind of business

Luís
So what brought you to Portugal? What was the temptation?

Taliesin
Has she a name, the Goddess of travel? I spent decades
in her service, jet-zagging oceans you bold Lusitanians
were the first ever to map. Whatever money I made,
I spent in her cause, that ripe-breasted anonymous one
who hides below the horizon. But all this time, my alert
Carapinha was at my side, and at last I respected her counsel.

Luís
I used to wonder what family feuds left the land you occupy
abandoned. Grapes soured on vines run wild, apples
rotted on the unmown grass, and the thousand year old
watercourse I drank from hunting sparrows as a boy, all
shouted for someone to unblock and harrow and prune.

Taliesin
What was I to do? She found the land yearning, and it matched
a need in ourselves. I tracked down my silk-tied fogy
with a bank to make profitable and mortgages on offer.
Twelve times a year my account bleeds, and in this fifth
age of my manhood, he lets me pretend I'm a farmer.

Luís
You lucky cuckolder! So a mortgage grants title to what's
not truly yours? Well, you're free to enjoy our dispossession.
It's not the most fertile land, no long-abandoned vineyard
is, but it's well-watered. The apple and pear trees cast

cool, rotating shadows. You can line up your hives
where the *canna* glows in the sunset, and no swallows
will swoop to catch the returning bees. Your arched
vines will yield you ample wine, your she-goats the ripest
cheeses. Take your olives to Diogo's press, and your corn
to be stone-ground in Pedro's windmill. Otherwise, you
need no one, save your lovely Carapinha, with her chickens
and her pigeon house, and the flowers she likes to fill
your house with. I admit I never planted flowers in my life.

Taliesin

Yet sooner shall Greeks and Turks mingle across
their common frontier to share each others wives, than
I'll regret my encounter with that entrepreneur in a suit.

Luís

But we others must pack up, like those east Europeans
migrating here, we must scatter where there's employment,
to England, serving from menus that appal us, to Germany
fighting Turks for a wage below the minimum, or home
to Africa to run some bottle store, though that's risky
business for our old skills aren't respected. No point being
homesick. Childhood's a different valley, made alien
by *novos ricos* who never milked a she-goat, or rubbed
well tilled soil between thumb and fingertips. No more
shepherding for me. To such a pass has the revolution brought us!

Taliesin

Luís, you're welcome to spend this night as our guest. We've
a Welsh roast with apple and chestnut sauce, and robust
Torres Vedras wines along with an active cheese. Look,
the sun's sinking. The pine trees' shadows have doubled.
Smoke is furling from the first of this winter's fires.

Trees again

Around where I now have purchase
are so many abandoned trees,

once integral to the small farms'
hoe-to-mouth economies,

orphaned by the developers
who move in with their bulldozers

and I wish I could adopt them.

The mossy dry-stone walls,
the water-courses and the wells,

the donkey tracks, the sheep pens,
are rubble in an afternoon,

but the odd tree on the computer-
mapped Byron Village print-out

is allowed (heavily lopped

and transplanted) a stunted heritage
as architect's camouflage

for the lack of virtue in what's deflowering
what was here before,

and I wish I could adopt them.

Ourique

Ourique on its eminence, that hot November
Sunday, seemed abandoned. We looked outwards.
On the parched plain to the horizon, each
cork oak loitered in its pool of shadow.

Back in the square an old man rose, drank
from the fountain, and sat without turning.
Empty alleyways, their cobbles polished
to pewter, zig-zagged steeply to the church

past the town hall where Camões's chiselled
octavos told of the battle that possibly
was fought here with a list of the heroes
who perhaps won. My whisper, translating

this, rattled like grapeshot. An orange
dropped audible, rolling in its gold foil
all the way down to the new by-pass,
though only we were around to record it.

The Platform

John's 19th birthday barbecue
the week before they both depart.
The platform by the old plum tree
that once hurled me to the ground's
yet to be tiled, but no matter.
There's the sound of running water
and a concrete base for tables and chairs,
the charcoal's already tinkling,
and for the first time we can see the spot
Alice chose gets the last of the sunset.

"Haven't you got a light down here?"
says Francisco, protesting the obvious.
By the time the spare ribs are done
it's starlight, and the peppered chicken's
served blindfold but delicious.
There's a good wine and cold beer,
we huddle in the slight chill,
and Alex indulges to the full
his drinking half and opening another,
as we toast John and celebrate his brother.

The looming wall of invisible canna's
a jagged tear at the sky's edge,
to the west, pines are silhouetted,
and revolving above us, in this
breeze from the furrowed Atlantic,
this out-of-town blackness, are
Orion and the Great Bear,
the Plough and distant Pleiades,
conspiring with the hour hand
that returns our sons to England.

I confide to Alice, "We create
the stage on which they play out
their departures, nothing more."
But for her, land, ancestors
and inheritance are not oases
on a desert journey, but
the beginning and purposed end.
Each shared meal, every heeled-in
root is like the northern star: a lantern,
a fixity, a magnet, and a legend.

I remember the exodus and the psalms,
the antipodes of my childhood:
the straight and narrow pilgrimage,
the annual round of milk and honey.
Like it or not, they are on their way
and their visits will be seasonal,
Christmas, and familial summer,
as the other loyalties we pray
will be theirs exert their tidal pull,
delivering other ceremonies of survival.

Fado

When Vasco da Gama captained Benfica,
those were the glory days. Vasco led
from the back, with Nick Coelho as keeper,
and his brother Paulo as inside-forward,

and Leonard Ribeira, an old-fashioned winger
(except when eyeing the girls in the crowd),
and the sprinter Fernão Veloso as striker,
with Diogo and Álvaro, all proud to wear red.

Those were the times of adventure and clout,
with Dom Manoel our manager-trainer
and Peru de Covilhã our roving scout.

Today we're trophy-less, bankrupt and disdained,
longing for Sebastian, cresting some tidal wave
on his surf-board, to alight in the Algarve.

Some Silicon Heaven
(for. António Rui, d. July 2002)

1

An African grief, with its harrowing
rituals, its staged spontaneity, its
strictly ordered wailing, the men
stern-faced, the women
out of control, yet
queuing for their moment, while

beyond all in the cramped apartment,
the TV crooning, the hi-fi
on maximum, as though here
in Lisbon, far from
likuba drums and the ecstasy
of dancing, something

rhythmic and cacophonous
has to be hurled in death's
maw – though Rui of all men
would have welcomed
professionally his obsequies'
punctuation by mobile phones …

2

Some lower the dead
into the earth;
the final instinct is growth.

Some place the dead
on funeral pyres,
fire to ash and fertiliser.

The truest burial's
at sea, all at sea,
salt tears, inconsolable.

3

The burial was simple, the coffin
opened at the graveside for final
cold kisses, then plunged no more
than a metre down, divided by less
than half that from the fresh grave
to the left (n° 548), and from the first
of five holes to the right, awaiting
the corpses queuing up behind us.

A plain ceremony in the municipal
cemetery at the municipality's
expense. Grim to leave Rui so
close to the surface, "in sure and certain
hope of the resurrection". The priest
strode quickly away, his robe flapping.

4

Rui, born in the *bairro*, father unknown,
with a cleft palate, a game leg, and sores
                              corrupting his eardrums,

213

would hobble the tracks between tin-roofed shanties
where women sweated at mortars or dragged behind them
                              huge water barrels,

with a watch strapped to his left wrist, a transistor
clapped to his right ear, gold teeth smiling, his shades
                              reflecting coconut palms,

and jabbering, stammering in tortured Portuguese
of a Grundig next year, a Suzuki, an outboard motor,
                              a Boeing 707 to Lisbon,

and we shared the joke. What worked and gleamed
he worshipped. People being flawed irreparably,
                              gadgets were his ikons.

5

So the censored version of what I published
years back, in the glee of discovering
he'd made it to the Grundig and Lisbon
being "voluble with images as ever". But

"his township mother" who was "always,
grinned the white managers, available
if you were desperate", is before me now
in the desperation of her grief, the one

lady left here Alice can speak with
in her mother tongue, and I feel shame
at something that teases and eludes.
Nothing I wrote was untrue, in praises

to celebrate his arrival. But Death
the Leveller promotes, and Rui's

departure chastens. He was
so sure he'd made it, absconding

from the girl he'd made pregnant
all those years back in Marromeu,
to the cramped ring of social
housing, and his *mulher da terra*.

Our friendship stood on the fallible
premise he amply reciprocated,
that his life was one long joke.
I've other friends who say this,

none who lived the part so fully.
Now his narrow cell imposes
its strictures, and I wonder
by what right I become his poet,

some ambivalent means of getting out
being all I ever contributed
to the countries I tried to help,
and he secured that without me.

More fitting the albums of sepia
photos, the annual masses sung
to a god he loved to ridicule,
the municipal headstone, the videos

with their countless, milling extras,
that extended, unregistered family
cramped in the box his widow
inherits the common-law right

to occupy, these are his legacy,

215

more than any words of mine
penned in by the truth he will
never again be uncontainable Rui.

6

In my sober dream, the motorway
continued. I had missed the turn-off,
then all turn-offs ceased, with all

road signs, petrol stations, cafes,
toll booths, just the concrete
rolling onwards through a misty

countryside with a brimming river,
and huge trucks and pantechnicons
racing both ways, three abreast

on the dizzying five chain curves
but never colliding, just waltzing
marvellously, free as skylarks

from the five senses and motion's
laws, and the dear lately dead
driving, wholly with us, uncorrupted.

7

So uncoffin him, let's celebrate his life!
He'd nothing, yet what he made of it beggared
                              all I have to offer.

Books, career, responsibility, investment, none
stretched so far as his world. Cable
                              TV did,

but only as a shining, channel-hopping box.
No programme, not even football, ever gagged
                                    his flow of commentary.

With invention, he suffered no handicap.
A poet, then, re-claiming the world,
                                    with the knack

to impose his dialect, in answering
which unwittingly all of us mimicked
                                    his impediment.

We never quitted his stall without
indulging his newest rhapsody
                                    of a Concord flight

to some silicon heaven where the latest-
bred clones have interchangeable
                                    body parts.

So invent on, my dear dead friend,
in the lives of those you gave ballast to,
                                    and count me in.

Suddenly, there's a new noise in my life

with a different rhythm.

It comes from the soak-away under the pine trees
beyond the stone wall in Pasqual's plot,
and it's called croaking, though

no sound's more bullish, more pulsing with semen than
this
throaty chuck chuckle, this guttural
rasping on a rising fifth, swelling at the larynx
like a condom, and ending in a whoop.

I'm coming to know Pasqual's frogs,
like we know our individual wren.

"That's Kermit", we say at first light
with his oink oink and purring whistle,
then Baron Scarpia abandons snoring
for his bass bassoon and kettle drum
to the wren's sweet piccolo,
a surer reveille than Amadeu's rooster
hallooing half the night.

Croaking, is it? I'll show you croaking.
From my wheelchair by the kitchen door
when whatever it is
is no longer operable,
I'll grunt my poems, *Vissi d'arte*,
while Pasqual's frogs supply the treble.

On the Run

This wren, this half-sparrow
with no neck, its tail stuck on

like a feather in the cap,
has commandeered our veranda,

startling us from sleep
with its trills and warbling, a looping whistle,
                    and nine rounds of rapid chatter.[3]

I draw the curtain an inch, and it's there,
chest tight as a ping-pong ball, lower beak rigid,

then a quick fire vibrato with oscillating shrills,
tail quivering like a baton

as it boasts to the valley,
This is my territory.

We know it from all the other wrens in the orchard.
That's ours, we say, no need to look round

from sowing onions or watering the lily bed.
This wren has us on the run.

---

[3] In *Guia de Aves: o guia de campo mais complete das aves de Portugual*, ed. Killian Mullarney et.at. (Assírio & Alvim, 2003), p 254, the wren's song is transcribed as follows: zitrivi-si **svi-svi-svi-svi-svi** zivüsu **zü-zü-zü-zü** si-**zirr-rrrrr svi-svi-svi** siyu-**zerrrrr** sivi

From the day it first intruded
with a beakfull of lichen,

the chairs, the flowerpots,
the tiled table where I draft my poems,

have been strictly off-limits,
as this womb-shaped nest incubating

the tiniest of the frailest
has us fretting, after

Freddie, Jean and George gone,
why we feel so chosen,

why in heaven would it matter
so much if he let us scare them off.

Against Reflection

The first time the rioting peasants
stormed into the Governor's
ivory palace, they stopped short
at the full-length looking-glass. Never
before, in forest pools or the missionaries'
mirrors, had they seen themselves
whole, red-eyed, with cow dung braids,
their pangas menacing their reflection.

Me, for example, my glinting panga
curving to the shins of this *canna*,
wellies, pants, torn shirt, disdaining
levis or shades or a straw hat, as

each professional day I scorn
tie and briefcase, in my refraction
of classlessness. Once mirrors
enter your life, there's no end to it.

Mimesis: imita-making, of course,
but the props of what's worth
inventing shift. We are in a garden,
more precisely, a garden in a poem.
Not that I'm cheating, it really exists
out there, beyond the arches,
I could show you around with pride
and pleasure, pointing out ...

but here's the argument. Having
indicated the garlic bed need
I, now it's in the poem's mirror,
bother watering it next day?
The book about the garden's
done, my latest re-baptism,
and the house, the authentic
metaphor of her who designed it.

Narcissus, Echo's toy boy,
pined away in self contemplation,
and she, too, faded, so that
all that survived was a cadence.
Something has root in me that
longs to shatter the looking-glass
to somewhere aboriginal, as at last
in middle age I turn romantic.

Morning Glory

Morning Glory dawns china blue
and all day following the sun
subtly changes register,
going out in a blaze of purple,

and every morning, May to November,
unfailingly there are fresh blossoms
following the same course,
sky blue to the original bougainvillea,

a day's life from the colour of ice
to the colour of the pine tree's long shadow
on the pantile earth of summer:
I'm glad I recorded this.

Moon-Struck

Octo-ber's the 10th month,
and today belongs to Thor;
we flag this as autumn
though cicadas are shrilling
"Out! It's time to plant."
The words, and what I do,
are adrift from where I began,
and from where I live now:
all my life it's been so.

The ninth's the 11th month,
and Venus eats her friend fish.
The armistice is St Martin's summer,
warm enough for bathing, though

the gods are at loggerheads.
All my life it's been so;
poets, said Yeats, should be
good liars, but must I
write in praise of November?

The Son's is the Sun's day,
and Dec-ember's the 12th:
daffodils hoist their bugles
among windfall oranges.
I've followed where the poem led,
I wake, make love, I eat,
I write – everything's a quotation.
So it's been, unchecked, as
few of the words connect.

A sheikh planted almond
trees for his Christian princess
who yearned for her snow.
Now two-faced Janus
inaugurates the year, this
day being moon-struck,
I start again, knowing the date's
wholly arbitrary, yet
eager for its harvest: there's
broad beans to be plucked.

The Catch

These 21C signs
are already out of date;

writing makes them out of date,
while writing of writing imposes closure,

yet re-visiting Ericeira
en route to an excellent fish lunch,

my post-modernist friend was driven to enquire
What are those terracotta pots for?

The fisherman, painting his tiny, ocean-
risking craft, concentrating

on the thin blue beading
of the window frame, said:

The octopussies like 'em.
and we catch 'em.

The Crocodile Poet

My nephew dropped by and we shared a bottle,
he impressed I'm some sort of bard,
I that he's a crocodile farmer,
his reptiles taking 9 years to breed.

The poet Horace (in Pope's translation)
praised the *9 years' pondered lay*,

describing not my pimply adolescence
but poems incubated for 3,000 days.

Here the metaphor wobbles. My nephew's
a living to earn, and can't afford
the crocodile's 9 years' pondered etc.,
so he takes to the swamps in dugout canoes,

raiding their nests for his supplies
while a hunter keeps the females subdued.
I wanted to say poems don't come easier
but it felt unworthy, so I refilled his glass.

Retirement Project

A friend, shockingly
grizzled for his years,
roars up like some
Hell's Angel and finds me,
scythe in hand, descending
the spiral staircase
to its basement storage
after summer use.

Cicada, old Tithonis,
your calendar confuses,
you chirp both spring
and autumn's planting,
and since my trajectory's yours,
given declining powers,
what the devil are you about
with all your shrilling?

And what matter is there
for further verse?
For a fresh book, must
I change wives, enlist
for Iraq, devise
the perfect murder?
How does the pastoral
poet stay in business?

Yet I've still not written enough
about how these pine candles
trail their pollen
to the breeze before
wheeling to November's scimitars,
or how that blue-gum at dusk
is utterly out-compassed
by the deeper night of this olive.

My friend roars off, his
retirement project
to be photo-ed at Europe's
compass points, yours
truly being furthest west.
A delicate manoeuvre
this, hoicking a scythe
down a spiral staircase.

Do Not Go Gentle

is a young man's poem;
it was his own death he raged against,

"going" too soon after. But rage
and age are siren rhymes,

and no one cares about an old man's anger.
The trick's to keep things light, as

this three score years and ten business
lets you watch those who upstaged you

be upstaged in their turn. Knowing,
meanwhile, far more than the kids who are,

you're no longer in charge of things,
so are called upon to be wise,

a word I never took seriously
till I found it means a man whose jokes,

exhumed from a lifetime's plagiarism,
the young repeat as their own.

Going gentle's indeed what I advise,
leaving behind some decent recipes.

Saints' Days

On Saints' days, July and August,
in these towns huddled along the Atlantic coast,

fishermens' wives before the sun is up
flock to the tiny chapel on the cliff top

and receive from the priest the waist-high image
of *Our Lady of a Safe Voyage*,

processing with her to the harbour
where their men have already appointed the honour

whose vessel *Nossa Senhora* will pilot
that day as the familial inshore fleet

rounds the breakwater and puts to sea.
There's never much trawling done that day,

just enough for a sea-fresh *caldeirada*
washed down by a good red from Bairrada

They show *Our Lady* their fishing grounds
where Ricardo and young Hélio drowned,

where the currents are worst on a rising tide,
and the choicest crayfish and octopus hide,

where they lay their nets in a half-mile arc
for tuna, and three kinds of shark,

or risk all, casting in the shoals,
chasing the mackerel or sardine schools.

They don't leave off till they're content
She's taken on board all that's meant

by men's work – not like the priest
their wives are wed to, that *holy ghost*!

At dusk, still steered by *Nossa Senhora,*
the little trawlers head for harbour,

each brightly lit from prow to stern
with multi-coloured bulbs and lanterns

a rich necklace, shimmering in the bay,
then dividing, each boat to her buoy.

On the breakwater and along the promenade
and the jetty, waiting to applaud,

are mega-families of market traders,
clerks, shoe-shine boys and waiters,

the old remembering days at sea,
the toddlers in Catholic finery.

lawyers, cooks, teachers, receptionists,
policemen, farmers, and footloose tourists.

Wives greet the fishermen on the strand
blessing the image from their hands,

and restore her to her chapel niche
until next *Our Lady's* inclined to fish.

(Matters like these I record in doggerel
to keep disbelief alive and well.)

Loudspeaker

(i.m. Melita Harris, a.k.a. 'Astra', d. 1 January, 2007)

1

After a funeral the collapsed star
would have gloated over – the peacock
crowd, the limousined ambassador,
the mourners' procession past her
cramped apartment block, the coffin
draped in Mozambique's flag (rescued
finally from the grave diggers),
here we are exchanging kisses
and she cold in the earth.
                              Burials
are swift here. As jet flight
between continents leaves
imagination stranded, death
shocks with its efficiency,
                    and mourning lags.

2

'"A heart attack", swears her husband,
returning from the new year's
fireworks, though neighbours assumed
ambulance and police were called
for yet another wife-beating,
Cape Verdean style. So we ex-pats
                    gossip.

3

Impossibly pretty, with her cat's
eyes and restless hips, she had
too many "protectors" in that colonial
sugar town. If the puffed features

and stocky build, that burgeoned
all too swiftly, had been there
from the start, she might have gained
schooling and family, but when
the coup heralded Independence, and she
could sing her way to the top,
the 'little honey' became Astra
                              and abandoned.
An image stays, of a braided-hair
festival, of exiles happy to be exiled,
or reconciled to exile, or homesick
beyond bearing, commemorating
AFRIKA, on a podium with batteries
of loudspeakers, and Astra bellowing
into the black lollipop her pastiche
of Makeba's *Uile Ngoan'a Batho*
– her infant daughter, wailing,
trying to clasp her thighs as
                      the audience laughed.

4

She was not quite famous, her talent
spread ever more shrilly as her body
thickened, and the town she'd rebelled
against faded in its death throes
to a golden city mourned. An uncivil
war bequeathed to taboo-inured
children, enacting nursery tale
horrors, made that older disorder
seem benign. So she ended refugee
from the liberators who promoted her,
singing to other nomads at ceremonies
of regret (come the truce, those same
exiles turned an overseas community,

231

with Astra its voice). If we grieve
for Melita, it's because her sexy
half-life, disdaining all purchase,
was somehow right for the age.
Her audience, however discriminating,
was always a hundred times mine
as "the struggle continues" became
the only enduring words. AFRIKA
you need loudspeakers, making
the most of the little left you,
and some sort of guiding star (like
that wailing daughter, today
                    studying law).

So Much More

City life's no big deal
– assuming you've a pad,
a job in some service industry,
a supermarket handy, a rag
to tell you what's in fashion:
kids can do it blindfold,
plugged into some simple gadget
playing even simpler lyrics.

My neighbour Amadeu, the farmer,
like any villager in Africa,
needs to know so much more.

Harvesting Courgettes

We're stuck indoors as these June storms
queue from the Atlantic, and our
courgettes are hourly more tumescent.
It's like we fed them with Viagra.

Does it hurt to be a courgette?
That spam I trash daily by the hour,
offering me four more centimetres,
has nothing on what's happening out there.

Dying Betjeman, interviewed in his wheelchair,
said on camera, "I didn't get enough sex"
(it's been expunged from the video).

But, as the tabloids know, the plain facts
are, all old men are dirty old men. So,
in my raincoat, the harvesting's my affair.

End-rhymes

"Exuberant arthritis"
is the X-ray diagnosis

of this pain in my toes,
shooting along the metatarsus,

and I'm delighted the illnesses
attendant on my age take

such pleasure in their work.
Better's to come, for sure,

some contentedly maturing
cancer, or jubilant thrombosis.

Padre Pedro's Cassock is Black[4]

This *Padre Pedro* red wine,
globalized in Bristol's
city centre M & S,
with a label Jilly Gooldening
its straw fresh bouquet,
with damson on the palate
and an aftertaste of the cigar box,
to be drunk in good company
with the best beef, or a nut loaf,
or cheese ripe enough to take it,

comes from vines implanted
in the baked alluvial sands
of an easily-missed village
on the nether bank of the Tagus.
Most farmers there opt
for Italian plum tomatoes,
not bothering to stake them,
the scarlet eggs ripening
on the level dunes by the million,
and these cross-bred grapes,
lower-slung than normal,
blacken fiercely
in the sand's eddying heat.

[4] A Batina do Padre Pedro é Preta , a popular tongue-twister.

To buy a case of twelve
you park by the *Adega*'s
portico, crossing the courtyard
with its panels of blue tiles,
kicking your heels while
a clerk from another era
shoulders down a ledger book,
inscribing with a fountain pen
the terms of your transaction.
You pay cash (no cheques
or plastic) and your receipt
is handwritten. A black man
with a trolley wheels
your case of wine to your car.

These bottles have other
labels naming the *Castelão*
grape, the strict temperature
of fermentation, the ageing
in barrels of Portuguese oak,
and the *terra podzolizada*,
Brazilian words for
alluvial soil, transported
in turn from the delta sands
of the River Zambezi, where
Podzo hippo hunters
relish their alternative *bife*.

This *Padre Pedro* black wine,
globalised in Cardiff's
city centre M & S,
is ignorant of its history.
If weekend ASBOs
in their dumb saturnalia

could be beamed down
to this inland delta where
harvesting peasants bend
low in their black hats,
and the priest in his black
cassock eats off a silver plate,
they'd see how it's matters
never brought to market make
the things markets trade.

> *Padre Pedro has a black heart,*
> *black is the heart of Padre Pedro:*
> *whoever says Pedro's heart isn't black*
> *has a blacker heart than Padre Pedro.*

Breaking News

Channel One's *Breaking News*
is a sloping beach strewn with wreckage,
with close-ups of a high-prowed boat,

its Phoenician eye squinting, its
timbers, with their primary colours,
splintered in the dawn surf.

Valhe-me Deus reads the taff rail,
reg. Nazaré, a fishing village
long swamped by a Tourist Board

in hock to the Euro. There's
journalists' babble the helicopters
were slow to respond, though

they were there before you reporters.
Then talk falls silent at an image
more ancient than anything I know:

three tall women in embroidered skirts,
their masculine faces half hidden
by the black cowls of their widowing,

shaking their fists at the wild Atlantic
and keening in words they alone use
– though who, even from a TV channel

between bouts of inane advert-speak,
has forgotten this elemental creole
when there's nothing more to lose?

The Balance
(i.m. Jill Dias, d. 28 April, 2008)

Some make their mark so gently
and without trumpeting, our mourning
feels chastened and constrained,

recalling less the brilliance than the courtesy,
the grilled sardines among Jill's flowerpots
with Alberto's best white Douro wines,

or those evenings in *Tasca* or *As Duas Amazonas*
where Alberto headed straight for the kitchen
to ensure his guests were never stinted,

so our arid hours in the Overseas Archive
or at the desks of the Geographical Society Library
where on the best days you'd run into Jill

and be guided through the bureaucratic maze
that opened at last on the thicker jungle
of that history she trod with the surest feet,

would culminate in a chilled bottle
on a wrought-iron table panelled with tiles,
in one of those glorious Lisbon dusks,

before the serious business of dining began.
So many tributes make clear my delight
was matched by so many, it's easily overlooked

how she pooled her knowledge, irrigating
the research of explorers from three continents,
and afterwards helping them into print,

how when our sardine-guzzling
is long forgotten, her work
will be cited as setting the standard.

She was hard at such work when her heart
attacked her, that warm heart her engine
under the sure conduct of her brain.

Constrained and chastened our grief
for Jill who always got the balance right
till bereavement smashed the scales.

That Enduring Delta

1

Dona Francisca, all purpose maid
to the sugar company's general manager,
belonging "to the better class of coloureds",

and awarded by the *Chefe* each rains
two corvée labourers to cultivate her plot
of mealies, pumpkins and sweet potatoes,

was as old as her century. At her birth,
slaves were still being marched in irons
to remote creeks in the Zambesi delta

for shipment in dhows to the Persian Gulf.
At 17, the year of the Uprising,
made sub-postal clerk in frontier Zumbo,

the lowest rung of the *assimilado* ladder,
she was swung by *machila*-bearers
(*Ona samuchende! Ona!*) half

the Zambesi valley, to take refuge
four sepia-hot days in a dugout
among exploding

heads of papyrus, until
the soldiers of both sides
had moved on.

2

Then Coetzee, who survived the Somme,
but not the Cape Town he returned to
with the white wife who screamed

he was black, trekked north
to these cane fields on the Zambesi,
and embraced his delta in her.

I met the octogenarian patriarch,
law-giver to a vast extended family,
when I was taken for his appraisal

one shimmering Sunday under his mango tree,
as we followed the tree's shadow round
with five litres of Dão wine,

completing the circle and the demijohn,
Yet none of those grandsons and daughters
were his own. The marriage, though

they were unmarried, was childless,
though their house swarmed with children,
as Dona Francisca adopted her tribe.

You could meet them all along the valley, marked
and their own children with her graciousness,
that has left its mark on me.

3

Like those islands in the sepia delta
that shape-shift with every flood,
she adapted to each imposition

240

as the rules changed around her.
To be white was impossible,
though her *nganga* had called her white,

to be black made no sense in her old age,
though she approved the revolution,
talking of that original Rising,

ending her days housekeeping
for the sons of one of those daughters.
So a stubborn current flows

from her life's domestic purpose
across that AID's wracked valley
where the counter-revolution has prevailed.

Indifferently, such rivers water
coconut palms, no two of which
twist with identical symmetry;

their ribbed shadows are like fish bones
in sandy creeks where watershed debris
blackens to rich alluvial soil.

6

from Letters from Portugal

Foreword

Language as metaphor was the original
take, which the linguists dodged
as too fuzzy for classification, tip-toeing
round the elephant in the classroom
in their hunt for the scientific rigours
of semantics, morphology, syntax, etc.
But I was happy with the imagination,
with nouns as names and verbs what
they were doing, anything beyond
(as Aristotle had said) being argument
by analogy, some uses of metaphor
outranking others.
                                    In the 80s,
all changed. Gingerly, linguists
began prodding that wrinkled hide,
tough as the outer-rind of a baobab,
while literary critics slumped
before an obsolete semiotics.
Language as signs was the mouse
to trap the elephant, as Shakespeare
lay down with bus tickets as matter
for serious study.
                                    30 years on,
linguists are still circling the beast
conjuring ever-more-desperate
neologisms for that prehensile trunk,
those tusks, those legs like mortars,
while the lit. crits., irrelevant
even to themselves as text finally

disappeared into context, flap away
in their sign-language behind doors
where no pachyderm ventures.

As for me, I'm sitting in a lecture
room, dark as always nowadays,
with a cloudy screen for attention, as
presenters hide behind their laptops.
But these cognitive scientists
are on to something, as they hack
a path through their own jungle
of synapses, qualia and NA+ions,
to a forest clearing with a sunlit pool
where the talk is of creativity, of Matsu
Bashô's haiku, as the elephant drinks
deeply and a frog melts in the water.

Letter 1

I must begin again by trusting, I *who*
always needed the five doorways,
only afterwards learning from the poem
the matter in my heart. So this dusk
my discipline is to water blindfold.
That hollow pattering on organ pipes
is the onion patch, that drizzle
on beach umbrellas the okra poles,
while the tomatoes are like spraying
a carpet till it hisses with saturation.
Drenched mint, thyme and basil respire
more pungently than in any cookbook.
I brush the bay tree and the scent

dusts the back of my hand till morning.
Then I open my eyes to the aubergines,
their purple sheen running with droplets,
the pimentos' crisp purses, the chillies'
scarlet toenails, as I shut off the hose
and open this blank page.

There've
always been different words for what
I write of. *Pinheiro*, three syllables
precise as their lengthening shadow
on the pan-tile earth of summer. Is
pine-tree the shadow of that shadow?
In a lifetime of travel, translation's
been the vehicle, as what's English-ed
becomes commonplace. Words like
picong, chimanga, nsondo, saudade,
ferried me tourist class to other worlds,
leaving me castaway with no link,
not even a hyphen, to the cramped
Baptist dialect of my childhood.

In a folded
spear of the Bird of Paradise lily,
two snails are mating. They began yesterday
and after twenty four hours' foreplay
are still at it, inserting mutual
penises into mutual vaginas. "In times
dedicated to universality and excess,"
I have "never been so interested
in very small things – twinkling tadpoles
in a barrel of water, the germination
of a fungus, ants nibbling at the leaves
of a lemon tree and leaving it like lace."[5]

[5] Estoban in Carpentier's *Explosion in a Cathedral*.

It's good to live where, as you return
from market with a rubbery fig shoot,
people ask "Where's it for?" as they
stroke the leaves lovingly. To sink
the roots of an olive sapling is to invest,
whatever the language, in millennia.
Step back after staking it, dusting
eloquent manure from your palms,
and history's fetch is at your elbow.

African Incident

Petrol gushes from the upturned tanker
down the dirt road in an African township,
dribbles past the road block and the bottle store,
is siphoned into the jerry cans of those nicking fuel

and explodes: three hundred are carbonized
with their loot, and in the breeze-block school,
and in the thatched compounds as the fire spreads
leaving blackened offices and a burnt-out market,

as oil once again stamps its carbon footprint
on the very poor – who need oil for their stoves
to make their root crops edible, all firewood
being exhausted by the weary columns of refugees

from war lords, whose deals with the conglomerates
that have carved up this darkening continent,
throw light on where this tanker was heading.
A long sentence. It matters that this is evil.

Letter 2

For 15 years, one of Lisbon's
sights has been that pastoral couple,
Florindo and Flora, keeping vigil
outside the Attorney-General's office.
Dependable as the rush hour, they hoist
their banner with its updated headline
4790 DAYS denouncing a JUDGE
and his BROTHER, a NOTARY, flanked
by photos of the cemetery in Aljustrel
where Florindo is officially buried.
He sits all day to the left, frowning over
a much-thumbed manual of basic law.
To the right, Flora salutes passers-by
and gossips with well-wishers.

                                    Born
in Nelas, close to the Dictator's origin
and home to a rough red *Dão* wine,
Florindo came to Lisbon at 10 seeking,
he says, "work". The war ended that year,
and somehow he flourished, putting
"two ragamuffins born in a tent" (that
Judge and that Notary) through school
and afterwards law school. His burial
certificate (prominently displayed)
says he "died in a foreign country"
and that travelling is our clue. Under
the Dictator, apart from the 50 families,
only emigrants made money, crossing
the border at night, dodging the patrols
and recruiters for the African wars.
If that's how Florindo prospered,
it was risky sending the profits home,

counting on gratitude from those
ragamuffin lawyers whose cunning
declared him dead and Flora re-married
(to invalidate her inheritance).
                    Midday,
June to October, they migrate to the shade
of the ruined mansion opposite, and in August
when Lisbon is abandoned they holiday.
They celebrate the saints' days
with citizens' goodwill. For the rest,
they are un-ignorably there, besieging
the windowless, cliff-like walls
of the Attorney-General's palace.
Eternally, the judges and the notaries
come and go.
                    Like so many countrymen
who spent decades paying for an upstairs
house called *The Emigrant's Dream,*
and came home to find the street deserted,
the school boarded up, the neighbours
of their childhood living in high-rise
flats on Lisbon's ring road, Florindo
found only on retirement he'd wasted
a lifetime investing in the Dictator's
delusion.
                    No decree will resurrect him
as he protests "until death". The fraud
exploited his truancy, no matter how
dictated, and the papers he spends his days
re-shuffling were long ago archived. Here,
where the best minds relish absurdity,
the pastoral has no voice. We
citizens, bidding good morrow
to our shepherdess and goatherd,

KNOW this is where we came from,
this is what we've been cheated of,
with no faith in where we're headed.

Recall your Purpose

Pity the ballad singer,
whether flattering kings
or praising the warrior
or consoling the wench
big-bellied but unwed,
while mocking the friar
who levied her maidenhead;

pity the ballad monger
when printing begins:
expelled from the court
by lordly sonneteers,
his pitch is the pavement,
as he rhymes of Newgate
to loitering servants;

pity the singer of tales
when he becomes folklore,
ancient turns of phrase
promoting ethnic wars;
song, recall your purpose:
*to burnish the other in ourselves
and ridicule all courtiers.*

Letter 3

Money defies gravity. It's man's
invention, at odds with the universe's
fundamental laws. It flows upwards
to the few with no delta in their heads.
When banks collapse, it doesn't spread
alluvial deposits over the millet fields
and rice paddies of the poor, but drifts
by veins and capillaries backwards
to clandestine vaults in Geneva.
Like H_2O money won't be incinerated.
It's the air we breathe, its fires are
never extinguished, it's the *terra firma*
we pace. Our invention owns us.
                              At
Tunapuna open market, Saturdays
by the railway crossing, I bought okra
and dasheen leaves from a bangled lady
in a shimmering sari. One morning,
she was late. She opened her bodice
and showed me the cause, nestling
like a lizard in the fold of her breasts,
the tiniest baby I've seen, delivered
in a roadside ditch on her 10-mile trek
to her roadside stall with a head load
of vegetables, and I felt shame
before the unplumbed stoicism
of the poor.
              This never required
translation, though I've needed
interpreters to bring to the printed
page those beyond history's reach:
Lal, unemployable, of no identifiable

descent, his subsistence inexplicable,
but crouched nightly over his tenor pan
the scion of perfectionism. Or Mamadu,
shovelling chicken shit, astounded his
hilltop shack was considered remote.
"Far," he exclaimed. "From where?"
Or Tomas Mbewe at the beer party,
dividing a chicken leg into equal
parts for the four excited children
at his knee. Or Emily Makua, who had
to borrow a cloth to speak with me
but who wouldn't admit she was poor:
with two surviving children (of eleven),
her life had been "blessed".

                    And yes,
I include in this catalogue those
traffic cops in Freetown, signalling
Stop and Proceed simultaneously,
to reap from whichever the harvest
of a bribe. At least their exaction
was witty and lucid – not language buckling
as hedge funds face a crunch of liquidity
with Iceland in meltdown, as Chrysler lacks
leverage, and sub-prime brokerage, fixed-
income arbitrage, and total return swaps
implode. No such thing as a free lunch?
Bankers are a bonus in this socialism
of the super rich. Money defies the gravity
of our instincts. It makes us stupid.

The Late-Born

Haunted by old faces, this long weekend
our house has echoed to much-loved nieces
and their impossibly naive husbands,

to toddlers in shoulder-harnesses
and the plastic paraphernalia of babyhood,
each securely the centre of its own existence,

and I at the periphery, a surrogate grandad
the kids are surprisingly content to escape
with from their parents' rubber stockade

to a jungle of ant trails and rabbit droppings,
mysterious feathers and puff balls for counting,
unlocked pine cones and a snaking hose pipe.

But there's something I know and they don't,
how that side-glance under a domed
forehead is an instant flash-photo

of the *nganga* her mother remembers
only in sepia, how that quivering lip as a finger's
bloodied by a thorn is that nephew, slender

at six, copied thrillingly in this youngster,
his exploring grandson. The much-mourned
crowd us in expression, dialect and gesture,
round this celebration of the late-born.

Letter 4

This has to be shared. In September's
gold dusk before the rains, before
cicadas shrill to announce the rains,
a nightingale perched on Pasqual's pine
is singing to nightingales who answer
from the forest. Impossible merely
to listen. I beckon Alice, and whisper
"*rouxinóis*". I summon Milton,
Coleridge and Keats, and declare "No
poet invented nightingales. Blot out
your *jug-jug* lines and listen."

                                For

decades I longed to write like Brahms,
in riffs more spacious than breath
can sustain. To write like a nightingale
requires the old forms, where lines
are sweetly self-contained, repeated
as the song, after little advances, rounds
on itself. Ballade and villanelle are the true
nightingale poems, the chorus echoing
from the forest – but already I'm
not listening. This songster knows
how to be still. After four seconds
of flute-like trills and intense, melodious
gurgling, come four masterly seconds
of nothing, echoing in the mind's
forest. Not a note revised, not a line
wasted.

        Out-staying the swallows
in this year's endless summer, they must
depart soon, crossing borders they don't
recognize with what needs no translation,

to the hungry generations of old Ghana,
Mali and Songhai. From cotton trees
shading thatched compounds, where griots
caress their bubbling xylophones with equal
economy, they will pour forth song
and silence. Such a nondescript bird
to make such a mark, both here,
and there in the withered savannahs
they are slow this year to return to. But
go, nightingales, go. This must be shared.

The Michaelmas Daisies

On the train linking the separate stations
of faith, religion, temple and clergy,
I leap off somewhere between
faith and religion, rolling
down the embankment
into a clump of michaelmas daisies,
their purple vestments glowing
in the November dusk.

Before Darwin, clerics found
evidences of God in nature.
Today, they discover God
in themselves, which seems
for all the eloquence
of the poetic divines
from Newman to Rowan Williams
a refraction too far.

Down line as it enters the tunnel,
I hear the train still hooting
and thank the liturgical simples
for halting my further fall,
resuming on poetry's sure
feet, untroubled by what's
unknowable, my journey
towards the ignorance called wisdom.

Letter 6

Walcott is inspired by train journeys,
the lines setting sure parameters,
but I challenge anyone to make poetry
from the sweaty scrum of airports
where nothing you feel about meeting
or parting translates to those hours
of cattle-herding.

Camões's,
favoured pun was *pena*, the quill
he wrote with and the plume he used
to transcend pain. He wrote of Phaethon,
scorching the city states of Mozambique
when Apollo's horses bolted. Icarus,
too, who fell from the sky into Auden's
nobly insouciant poem. Poets are wary
of soaring these days. The sublime's
for academics who want religion
without too much by way of belief,
or parade non-religion by killing off
authors, God being alive in Uruguay.
But we deserve a poetry of airports,

Miltonic or Dante-esque, grand style
or plain, the common element hell.
                            Who's
committing this affront of travel? On
who's authority? With what baggage?
Report to the gate. Be identified again.
Pace 25 metres to the left, 25 to the right,
this a dozen times until finger-printed
and retina-scanned, stripped of jacket,
belt and shoes, coin-less and key-less,
X-rayed and intimately body-fumbled,
you ascend to a paradise where every
sin is permitted – Pride that you're
in with the jet set, Gluttony at Harrods's
sweet-meats, Lechery drooling over
top shelf magazines, Envy the Versace
scarves are unaffordable, Greed filling
your trolley with duty free, Sloth slumped
before the flight indicator, Wrath at this
damned 5th Circle. Boarding at last,
you're instructed to belt-up and ogle
the hostess's figure-hugging uniform as
she moves like an Indian dancer, conjuring
what's no way to be faced.
                            Nothing,
cold-shoulders like air travel. Those stilt-
walking villages of the brimming delta
are hard to keep in vision, even as
the shape of poverty is chartered.
Precious people over-flown stare up
at our jet stream scribble. Far from
those highways inking the watersheds,
dirt roads circle teetering boulders
with their own scribble I could wipe off

with my sleeve. White-sand beaches
with their fishermen's dugouts,
scythed by the plane's shadow,
are shifting dykes between swamp
and tsunami. Our destination cities
are increasingly like airports. Besieged
by hills scarred red with shanties,
or by high rise dungeons on metropolitan
ring roads, they rattle in our wake as we
tilt for landing. Our captain "hopes
we'd a pleasant flight", reeling off height,
speed, temperature, time of arrival,
his numbers not Walcott's abacus,
just numbers

          As for Icarus
a.k.a. Yuri Gagarin, I derive
wonder (not the sublime) these days
from the *New Scientist*, not *Poetry Review*.
How come magnolias are pollinated by
beetles? How do we know pre-Homeric
cavemen were intermittent residents?
They evolved before bees. Their deposits
of bones and tools are separated by layers
of bat droppings. That kestrel rippling
on his thong of air has X-ray vision,
alert at 50 metres to a beetle's sheen.
Poetry can't match such news, its unique
virtue to keep us sure-footed, especially
when, as always, we're on the move.

Like a Bonsai Tree

The spade and the hoe,
cultural signifiers,
in hoc to the scythe.

Like a bonsai tree,
not a poem to cast shade,
just to contemplate.

Letter 7

"May I ask you a personal question?" I was
lunching with Paula and Vasco, and Paula
sprang this on me. "How personal?"
"Highly personal." "Go right ahead."
I expected something about my sex life,
or possibly religion, which in a sense
proved correct, though her actual enquiry
took me aback.

             "Are you a communist?"
I'm not normally stumped, but this cultural
miscue had me floundering. How explain
the gap between what I would surely
have been if born here, and what I am?
The question had a history. Before she
accepted Ricardo's proposal, she put
the same query and was told firmly, "*Não*."
Only after their son's birth, in a marriage
that has proved enduring, did he confess,
adding, "You wouldn't have married me
otherwise." He was right on both counts.

In those days, denying you were communist
was the correct thing to do, which made
her question to me unanswerable, at least
in Portuguese. "After Hungary '56,"
I ventured, "when droves deserted the party,
it was no time to be joining. In Britain,
membership was never illegal, only
signing up to the homintern" – but Paula's
eyes had glazed over.

                      Its cells
surviving Salazar's strict clericalism,
the PCP was icily Stalinist, yet
warmed by the faith of two generations
of the most talented. Lopes Graça,
Portugal's foremost composer, his study
cluttered with busts of Lenin presented
at innumerable East European festivals,
was a life-long member. Street crowds
at his funeral sang the music they loved
from his *Requiem Mass for the Victims
of Fascism*. Nobel-novelist Saramago
never tore up his party card. He took
the long view, writing with informed
devotion of Romanesque chapels. It was
when Brazil's gold furnished the frigid
contours of the Baroque, the rot took hold.
The *Estado Novo* was a footnote.

                    As for
Álvaro Cunhal, the dictator's glacial
doppelgänger, he de-iced in old age
as Manuel Tiago, best-selling novelist,
prison-translator of the *King Lear*
prescribed in *Estado Novo* schools,
and author of a fine book on aesthetics.

Given such company, the query "Are you
a communist?" seems high praise.
                                    Yet
I'm not, and in Portugal you don't
become one by conversion. Most
are born communist, in a culture
of CP-dominated family networks
in those regions with a history of revolt
against absolutism. It's like the reasons
for growing up Catholic, and just as
you can be lapsed catholic, people
would rather be lapsed communists
than abandon the party. Such politics
are very local, the enemy landowners,
tax collectors, priests and the army,
intruding on the autonomy of villages
best managed by the people themselves.
Vasco, our fellow diner, subscribes
in melancholy fashion to the far right
People's Party. In local elections, he votes
for the communist mayor whose social
programs he approves.
                                Will the PCP
survive without the opium of that
anti-fascist struggle? Its members
are aging, and with the drift to the cities,
local politics dwindle. Last year
in Setubal, at an open market close
to the port were a dozen bookstalls.
Polished-leather editions of Lenin
were piled up. I could have bought
the *Collected Speeches of Enver Hoxha*
for a song. Cherished items, once dangerous
to possess, looking for new homes.

262

Dialectic

Raised in the devout north
in that city with 21 churches,
when the man she would marry
first stared at Maria das Dores,
her instinct shuddered
he was of the devil.

Raised instead in the latifundia south where
landlords still exercised their seigneurial rights,
and the serfs (for so they were, as they queued
daily for occasional field work) were
anarchist in theory but admired Stalin,
when she first glimpsed the husband
of her life, entering that clandestine room,
her instinct trembled
he must be *PIDE*.[6]

Over the years, she bore the stigmata
of the wife of a jailed comrade,
deaf in her left ear from the blows
of an inquisitor who felt cowed by her faith,
raising the children conceived
in the intervals of his paroles,
till his death in Tarrafal[7]
opened the cell of her widowhood.

Unusually, they released the body
and she did everything that was correct,

[6] *Policia Internacional e de Defesa do Estado,* Salazar's political police
with a special record of brutality.
[7] The *PIDE* prison in Cape Verde.

keeping her all-night vigil
(for the dead must not be left alone),
celebrating the momentous
missa de corpo presente in a church
too cramped for the 1000s of mourners,
and leading them to the municipal cemetery
to cast the first handful of alluvial sand.

>   *Raised in the devout north*
>   *in that city with 21 churches,*
>   *when Maria das Dores*
>   *became pregnant by a man*
>   *she declined to marry,*
>   *she opted for an abortion.*

Letter 9

Sunlight, yellow in its winter angle,
gilds the underside of pine needles,
and half-moons eucalyptus boles
with their plasticine-coloured
shards. Last August's silver fish
are gold-leaf twirling to the ground.
Vineyards, ankle-deep in sorrel,
glow like skylights lit from within,
while sunlight flashes from the wings
of goldfinches, flocking in the latticed
bamboo, their polls scarlet
as rosehips.
                Yet another Xmas
survived! Another 24 hours'
New Year fireworks from Sydney Harbour

264

to N.Y. Times Square, and the last
in my lifetime to be countered by
returning to a job. But how shape-shift
at my age – I, for whom family and friends,
books, gardening and dining, peppered
by anger at the world's governance,
energise my calendar now the work
that justified me dwindles? "You're
hired to do a job," said Sir Frank,[8]
46 years back as I agonised about
poverty. "Your job's to do it properly".
Captain's advice that kept me steady
in a trade I've come to doubt.
The students I most influenced shared
my scepticism as they readied for exile,
while my scholarship is about people
whose pickings each harvest never
sufficed to buy the books. Yet until now
it's about to expire, only jailer Banda
ever suspended my licence to teach. Not
for me *Professor Jubilado*, who prefers
poetry's calibrated failure.
                              A robin
watches me prepare the kitchen garden
with chipped pine bark and leaf mould,
and I study *Senhor Pisco-de-Peito-Ruivo*
as he perches on my wheelbarrow's
handle, puffing his chest in the dazzle
of late January. Is he taking notes

[8] Sir Frank Worrall, first black captain of the West Indian cricket team
and most successful ever, a childhood hero who before his untimely
death I had the privilege to serve as a colleague in Trinidad.

for a poem, that robin kind where no two
riffs are identical? The pathetic fallacy's
his if he reckons he can learn from me.

Across the Valley

On my post-op. thrombosis-averting
constitutional, I glimpse from across
the valley between the wild figs and walnuts

her, watering the rose and lily beds
in this pale January sunlight
and, at this distance of forty years,

my heart and pacing stops. The sun
is low above the Atlantic for both of us
and the valley between, yellowing

after seven weeks of unseasonal drought,
is already dark. But she and I,
isolated figures, are picked out by the sun.

A moment, of course. I resume strolling,
she turns off the hose. The chimney's
already smoking as I approach home.

Letter 10

Foreign heretics like me used to be buried
(so the Inquisition graciously conceded)

in the sand at low tide, leaving no memorial,
but Catholic and Communist believers,
and we others, still gravitate to the beaches.
From mountain sheep-folds, canning factories,
stone-bordered farms, and high-rise apartments
we are drawn to the Atlantic's immensity,
as though in a country half of whose borders
are coastline, the land has no resonance.

                         No one
stares out to sea like a mid-life Portuguese,
his stomach folds embracing his beach trunks,
his scalp repeating the sunset. Even
this winter afternoon, as rollers advance
in parallel lines, each green breaker rearing
like glass before shattering in the undertow
of the wave before it, even in January,
you see him anchored in the tide wrack,
muffled against the west wind, his gaze held
by something invisible.

> *How simple it is to bury a man,*
> *any wave of the sea, any foreign*
> *mound, as with our friends, will accommodate*
> *flesh, no matter how lowly or how great.*

So Camoes' navigators, dying of scurvy
in the Zambezi delta, more Portuguese being
buried in the five seas or in the soil of five
continents, than here where the land ends
and the ocean begins.

                    On the Discoverers'
Monument at Belem, viceroys, navigators,
soldiers, priests, farmers with their ploughs,
João de Barros with his *Décadas*, Camões

with a stray stanza, all mount a prow opening
on a sea-borne empire. "Where's the merchant?"
I asked my history class. "Oh," nonchalantly,
"we left that to the Jews".

For there was always
more loss than profit in Portugal's version
of *exploração,* the noun merging exploitation
with the acquisition of knowledge in a trope
to make Foucault look *passé*. Palace-convents
were built by the same forced labour. The rest
was faith, a refracted vision of agency
in a divine purpose for the world consuming
generations of the peasantry, not to be shrugged off
(as did we heretic money-makers), but navigating
where the astrolabe took them until shipwrecked
by history.

My anonymous friend stares
at a sun soon to rise above Cape Cod. He and I
have more in common than you'd think
as he lets the backwash lap about his ankles,
hoping some driftwood might yet come his way.

A Show of Fine Words

The last exam I assessed
after 46 years of marking
time, a supplementary paper
on a subject about to be retired,
had the candidate's name and number
and the level he aspired to, and no
more, all five questions *em branco*.

I was tempted. It was my last chance
to arbitrate degree, and his satire
on my near half century's
professing seemed profound
– like *Tristram Shandy*'s
blank page, or the waiting
in *Godot*, or John Cage's *4'33"*.

Should I give him a First
for knowing how little we know
about anything? Or was it
he didn't know what we don't
know, so couldn't manage
a show of fine words?
(I awarded him, and myself, a zero).

Letter 11

April, and the vegetable patch
is water-logged. I've diverted
the stream running past it. I've sunk
walls of tiles along the perimeter. Today
three spade depths down, I unearth
a fresh spring spurting six inches
from the clay. Amid tomato seedlings,
onion shoots and the first twin petals
of pumpkin and cucumber, is a perennial
fountain, lacking only such conduits
as the first Berber farmers of this terrace
managed by instinct.
                              Sky TV's exposé
is of ferries, trawlers and ocean-going dhows,

sardine-packed like the old slavers
with migrants who've paid their bribe
to be smuggled into fortress Europe.
Before the Algarve became a frontier
bristling with patrols, their voyage
was routine, that River Senegal
their *talifa*'s southern boundary. Our
plot remains irrigated by translation –
azeitonas, the word by which I cure
olives, daily changing the brine, *enxada*,
Alice's hoe, *acequia*, the watercourse,
marked by the Moorish arch declaring
this division at the valley's head more
ancient than Portugal.

The toe-nail moon
of *Eid-ul-Fitr* slides above the tallest pine
and I think of Ibne Mucana al-Isbuni,
our neighbour a thousand years back
who sang of his agile sickle, and wrote
how "a glass of white wine sets you up
for Friday's prayers". He looked to Cordoba
and beyond to Baghdad as the fountain
of learning and culture. We *kaffirs*
at Coimbra's gates were his nightmare,
trampling his world of tolerant learning,
of the managing of light and water
and the delicate fall of a cadence,
like the wild pigs from Cintra mountain
that annually ravaged his corn.

"A man
of purpose," (his chiselled epitaph) "needs
a windmill turning with the clouds."
Those windmills survive him. The residue
was laid waste by austere tribes

from the Sahara, wielding the *Qur'an*
like scimitars. Then the Catholic
monarchs turned the encroaching waste
into their courtly hunting grounds,
and enlightenment was snuffed out.
Tonight, as *Eid*'s sickle moon sprints
through marbled rain clouds, it's
my luck of purchase to be managing water.

The Gift of Tongues

The wall is turning to face the sun,
it's *Dia da Espiga*, Ascension Day,
the holiest day in the calendar
when at noon rivers cease to flow,
the milk in the churn won't curdle
and loaves lie flat in the oven.

In Grão Vasco's *A Ascensão*[9],
we see Christ from the waist down
cut off, as his body floats, by the frame,
an image so majestically literal minded
it all-but commands credence in a Christ
torn in half between earth and heaven.

The wall is turning to face the sun,
as from high-rise balconies, old women,
dressed today like peasants, come down

[9] Vasco Fernandes, known as Grão Vasco, early 16C Portuguese
painter. His works are held at the museum named for him in Viseu.

with posies they've culled from somewhere
of marigold, vetch, camomile and poppy,
sprays of olive and of rosemary,

with an ear of wheat (the defining *espiga*),
each sprig an afternoon's metaphor
for peace, love, health and prosperity,
attainable, as we tired commuters
ascend on escalators from the metro,
for an austerely de-valued euro.

The wall is turning to face the sun,
Christ's head and heart are invisible,
his loins and feet being earthbound
in this baptized pagan festival
that heralds summer. On offer next:
cloven tongues, the gift of translation.

Letter 13

She is literate. She has an exercise book
and a biro. Her riposte to being gang-
raped on the mattress of her husband's
dismembered corpse, is to compile the record.
When other women bring her their tales,
she sets up a "Listening House" of sun-dried
bricks and a grass roof, where chickens scratch
and goats snuffle. At a Formica-topped desk
with a paraffin lamp, beside a dirt road
in the forest, she records what was done,
and what done next, and what was then added,
meticulously, horror by horror. Her pen

is not mightier than the penis. But writing
taunts these boy soldiers who themselves
cannot read and, hearing rumours of her
archive, rape her again in their weakness.
                    Behind
our own house, there's a patch still
unclaimed from builder's rubble.
It's where lorries manoeuvre, emptying
the cess pool or delivering manure.
Even in the rains, only fox-tail grass
gains a toehold, and under August's
blow torch, it's a 30 square-metre pan tile.
This is the month when ants mill
in kitchens and bathrooms, desperate
for water. They emerge between the tiles,
counting their steps to the sink or bathtub
and back, reckoning to the non-existent crack.
They climb chair legs to the table, swarming
across this manuscript. They march
in wobbly columns down the green
motorway of the hosepipe, or relax
in the plumes of well-hosed sweet corn.
Miraculous that on those thirty-square
metres of baked brick the ants avoid,
a watermelon has found purchase, with starfish
tendrils and tripinnate leaves, and already
sporting a Gaia-green globe.

                            It seems
blasphemous to conflate my joy in writing,
with hers in that hut in D.R. Congo's
darkness, the goats her only audience. "No
poetry after Auschwitz," intoned Adorno,
and her fierce witness makes Imagism
or calculated line-breaks seem stockaded

frivolities. Yet, in the shadow of the Shoah,
children danced and sang in playgrounds,
and the shoots of the lyric re-emerged
in a relentless forgetting. Writing, which
we don't inherit, transcending song
like the recording angel, is in the psyche
of all cultures. Like the holy graffiti
of death row, it defeats silence.
                    We pray
for when she in her listening house
welcomes the swallows after their brief
exile, as the signal to hoe her garden
for the rains. Even now they are circling
higher and higher, milling like ants, scenting
departure. Then she with her pumpkin seeds
and her maize (this is the time we pray for)
will have different matters to record. Along
with those other culture-building women,
in the various markets accessible by box-body,
the price of mealies, cassava, and bananas
will (this is truly what we pray for) backlog
their mobile phones, as their children clamour
for school books. If then they have time
for the sunset blaze of a pumpkin, or
the pony-tail of a ripe maize cob,
conjuring metaphor to ballast their joy,
I shall reclaim the right to write of them.

The Song Instinct

70 years of living
have been such a brief cycle,
the Bible's allotted span
bringing me full circle
to the blank child I began.

I could rhyme from the start:
now of all I thought I knew
through travel and travail
of the globe's many peoples,
there remains this scruple.

40 years of marriage
have been too brief a space
to cultivate the innocent skill
of holding another's happiness
in cupped hands without spilling.

30 years of publishing,
that narrowest of windows
when my words were
bound by the classroom,
have exhausted preaching,

leaving rhyme's echo
to tantalize – maybe
this time, this one book
will marry content
to form transcendentally.

10 years since together
we planted this garden,

we have watched trees
attain our stature
in days seeming without end.

The enclosing dry-stone
walls, with their calendar
of lichens, were cooked
and layered through
mindless millennia.

What will survive
of us are genes,
timelessly re-born,
transmitted like song
with nothing learned.

Letter 14

Across the ridges north of Lisbon
the windmills are advancing.
Alice says they march at night,
halting on one leg at dawn,
their three arms signalling
green insouciance: next day
they're on your doorstep.
                              So
it encroaches, whatever it is,
under so many isms. Even
Anastásio is planting illegal
beacons on my neighbour's land,
and his goats are vulgarly
imperious, fucking and gorging

and fucking and lecherous for more.
14 years on, the snakes are gone:
they were harmless and bejewelled,
and they're gone.
              I, an old man
in the planting season, as this
land's diminished before my eyes,
hurl from my tiled veranda
poems of defiance. I laugh with the goats.
I greet the rare hoopoe, my binoculars
misting with joy. That beaten-silver
snakeskin by the watercourse
is a trophy.
             There's a working
windmill we take visitors to see,
eight spars honed like a caravel's
masts, and roped in the fashion
of men who live by sail. Four
canvasses are spread to the Atlantic
gales, with clay pots lashed
to the rigging to give the windmill
a voice, the whole cogged to a spliced
piston that turns the three-quarter ton
grindstone within. What might
have reconciled Don Quixote
to this sea-borne technology had he
climbed the curved, floury ladder,
is the stately process of scissoring.
A thimble of grain at a time feathers
to the bedstone's socket, the powder
trickling with infinite gentleness
to the flour sack below. This miller
is both gale-mastering navigator
and furrowed-eyed engraver, and his

stone-ground mealies taste of when
five continents ate from the same
pot – a grain-based starch, a relish
of beans, leaves, or stewed game,
or that hard-as-concrete goat's
cheese Sancho Panza carried always
in his satchel.
                          Eternal knight
of the sad countenance, you'd have
spurred Rocinante to tilt your lance
at these ecological wind farms
dividing you from your Dulciana.
Your visionary poetry rebukes
me *who always needed the five
doorways*, knowing tomorrow's sun
will rise, even knowing no way
of knowing how I know it.

Two Voices

Two voices are at war,
one lyrical, watered by my travels,
one ironic, the childhood me.

On a sharpened quill
the poem soars
to be shot down by humour.

But what pleasure to regard a tree
lovingly pruned over the years
bent low with pears.

Afterword

Trusting language,
knowing most nouns
are metaphors,
and every verb
a conveyor-belt,
is a religion
of sorts, wired
in the brain.

In the beginning
was the Word,
and the God-words
are arsehole,
prayer, *chikonde*,
merde, along with
justicia, *nsondo*,
mercy, the sounds

alone arbitrary,
the syntax soldered,
the poet's god-like
cunning (if she knows
her craft) being,
not to be chosen
but, undeterminedly
to choose.

7

War Poets Revisited

Warrior kings are the stuff
of the oldest poems, the ones
written down afterwards. Metaphor
dissolves before their greatness,
as the sun halts, the moon calves,
the he-goat yields abundant milk.
Their largess is targeted, those skulls
over-flowing with mead and millet beer,
till the poem ends with a reminder
that the king's fame depends
on the poet, whose skills
are the pudding's proof.

The last time poetry mattered
was World War 1. For the historians
this matters. When else did four
years produce so much history?
Yet it's the poets, their vision
trench bound (actually "the safest
place to be") who've made all
the running, and no matter
how the revisionists argue
the Somme was just a sideshow,
Owen & Sassoon point the larger truth
with their capacity for myth;

which is why so many of my friends
are hankering to be war poets.
None of them's in any danger,
their most serious wounds
being benefit cuts. But while Gaza
is annihilated, and Iraq, Syria

and Libya burn, complicity
rhymes with the sheer futility
of poems of raging protest
at the profanities of war.
Alas, my friends, you're just
re-writing Owen. And he was there.

Carapinheira's St George (and the Dragon)

Alice recalls hippos surfacing from the Zambesi at dusk,
plashing across the rice fields to forage with loud snuffles
in the pumpkin patch and the maize gardens, undeterred

by the huge skulls posted along their usual tracks,
or by the women ullulating and banging cooking pots
with their ladles. She remembers the Zambesi in flood,

lapping the stilts of her mother's house, the snake
in the rafters her mother laughed at her for fearing,
and the curious incense she burned to drive it away.

She recalls sitting stock still in her *nganga's* village
while the gentle elephants, whose careless ambling
could crush granaries or whole compounds, made

their own way down to the Zambesi's bank. All this
she speaks of with love and gratitude, pouring out
beer and maizeflour in holy remembrance. But

this latest beast, emerging at night from the forest
to flatten, plant by plant, our rows of sweet corn,
shucking the kernels, leaving the dry purse intact,

this northern predator has her burning with outrage.
"What's this?" she demands, showing Lucas the debris
where only last autumn I forked in leaf mould.

"*Texugos*," said Lucas, the woodcutter, with a grin.
"They can destroy whole farms." "*Texugos*", she mutters,
bringing me the word. I type in Google Translate

and come up with *Badgers*. After three decades,
she's accustomed to skinheads, racists,
child-snatchers, rapists, UKIP, journalists,

shopkeepers dubbing her hen, duck or pet,
paedophiles, house-breakers, phone hackers, the police,
as the customary hazards of living in Europe, but

these creatures drawn by starlight to target
with corkscrew precision one of her favourite foods,
these *badgers* (bad buggers?) are a presumption too far.

"They avoid humans," says Lucas. "*Meias suadas*
are all that's needed to keep them at bay." Alice's
St George is well past retirement, but sweaty socks

I can still supply, to repel this fiercest of her dragons.
Nailed to a post at the forest's edge, during next July's
harvest (and downwind from the house), they'll furnish

the latest mantling on the scutcheon of my love.

When the improbable has been eliminated

Last night we trouped to see *Casablanca*
with Ronald Regan and Hedy Lamarr.
Nice music, but the action didn't grip.
Who cares which of them boarded that plane?

Bogart turned out to be a great President.
"Here's looking at you kid" went down well
with Golda Meir, averting at the last minute
a war whose days were about to be numbered.

Imagine a world where the Israelis sponsored
Hamas, where the CIA armed Osama bin Laden,
and the British gave chemicals to Saddam Hussein.

The truest poetry is the most deceiving.
When the improbable has been eliminated,
what's impossible has to be the key.

In Praise of Marriage

The pine tree heaves slowly
in the full blast of the Atlantic storm,
its massive boughs tempering
the buffets of wind and golf ball hail.
Its twin trunks are like stately dancers
bound in an elderly embrace
as the storm is shouting. It will blow
itself out before the dance is through.

To find yourself in your opposite
is one definition of marriage,

not a search for fulfillment
in self-asserted identity,
but a tempered journey of discovery
with no destination but old age,
having each anniversary
learned more, there being forever

more to take in about your partner's
difference. It helps (my synthesis
of wisdom) you had from the start
not much in common. Many a groom
have been ship-wrecked, wedding
the girl next door, assuming
the local dialect was shared
by a woman with no talent for surprises.

Take Mike and Amina – he crushed
by rancorous divorce, finding
in Malawi academic asylum,
she his new garden boy's sister
abandoned with seven children.
Within a month they were married.
Today, she and the seven are graduates:
it took merely the embrace of opposites.

As the Atlantic sky begins to clear
the pine trunks, like some legendary
lovers metamorphosed in Ovid,
maintain their sarabande of minims,
their candles trailing pollen.
How many rings do the trunks share?
Our own is a single band of gold,
gleaming in its fifth decade.

Funk Rap

To create, so I read, *a sense of futility*
in uncooperative detainees,
the damned souls of Gitmo *are played*
non-stop Britney Spears.

Noriega, narcokleptic bum,
blasted by *I fought the law*,
funk rock classic at Arctic volume,
surrendered to his supplier.

It's good to know Michael Jackson,
Geldorf, Boy George, Bono & Jagger,
are always available to torture
America's enemies into line.

So might the inquisition's Torquemada
have finally convinced the Jews
not with wheel, rack and thumbscrew
but twenty-four/seven Madonna.

Africa's Gift

Acedinhas or Little Bitters, (botanically
a type of sorrel), November to April

they're everywhere with their trefoil
leaves and long-stem cowslip bells,

infesting pastures, crofts, gardens
and veranda flowerpots, a weed

288

in fact, whose birdcage of stalks,
mounting above our early bulbs,

I yank out by the handful, to leave
white spores like ants' eggs

to spring infallibly next rains – after
migrating from the Cape of Storms

in the baggage of some navigator,
some clone of Bartolomeu Dias,

or in the mud of his ankle boots,
they've taken over like this sentence,

impossible to pause or parse,
able to poison entire flocks

of bloated sheep, and yet a marker,
reliable as St Martin's Summer,

a gold carpet in the pruned vinyards
at the year's decline, Africa's gift

to our winter, dangerously lovely.

Riddle

The history of that land is
no Roman set foot there
    the turbulence of rivers
    not being history.

The history of that land is
they did not invent the wheel
    the baobab's elephantiasis
    not being history.

The history of that land is
they had no sacred texts
    conjuring the first rains
    not being history.

History discovered them,
spiriting away their past
    today their stories
    are of dispossession.

Climacteric

1

Those October dusks we shared on the veranda,
staring across the valley at our smallholder neighbours
as electric cicadas heralded the rains,

are history. Atlantic storms are forecast,
but cicadas don't watch television
and no plant nor animal knows what's going on.

Blue tits, caught in translation's paradox
(the 10th named the 8th, but taken to be 4th),
are checking out April's nesting boxes.

The gooseneck cactus opens at midnight,
broad and white as a dinner plate, as though
August's full moon had never quartered.

The almonds I must prune before January's
lace are already in bud. Should they blossom
while the bees are hibernating, what next?

2
Mosquito, mating with itself in the bathroom mirror,
is disturbed by the image of the poet shaving,
so zig-zags to drone-bomb my left ear,

while I flap ineffectively with my free hand
and succeed only in cutting my chin.
I grabbed them almost invariably once,

but I'm slower now, or perhaps they're nimbler.
It was, after all, the 10% that survived
went on to breed, over more generations

than I've fathered, giving them the genetic edge.
Leaving climate change out of account,
which brings more and more of them northwards

with their dread cargo of cerebral malaria,
I'm losing the evolutionary war, especially
with insects, most of all those after my blood.

So let mosquito brain-fuck his reflected self
while I'm careful to shave unobtrusively,
a tactical gain in a battle long since forfeit.

3
Our ancestors' satisfaction at graduating
from hunting and gathering to subsistence
farming was surely mixed. Was it the women,

tired of a peripatetic life, who insisted
on settling down, seeing how the edible
grasses they plucked for pounding rusted

annually in the same patch of veldt?
Or was it the men, determined to bring these
wanderlust wives under better control

in more manageable little societies,
who handed out the digging sticks?
Whichever, we can all rejoice

they'd already learned how to walk erect,
freeing their hands for what hands do
and with 3D vision to detect snakes,

for 50% of agriculture's done
on one's hands and knees, as sowing,
weeding and harvesting impose bending;

otherwise, we'd maybe never have known
about gazing at hills or distant oases
(or enjoyed the missionary position).

Nor need farming the land (pacé Rousseau)
have meant planting the first fences.
All it took, as I annually witness

here where I've put down roots, is the sense
that what you plant and reap is yours.
No one pilfers a crop, out of reverence

not for property but for the human labour,
whether or not there's a ditch or a wall,
or the presence or absence of barbed wire.

4

These, though, are peasant conundrums.
What of Katrina's or Sandy's victims,
or the rapidly drowning Maldives,

while Alaskan ice-floes await their first
oil-drenched polar bears? Now those neighbours,
once our avatars of seed time and harvest,

are gone, our plot's original Moslem calendar
tempts with its lucidity. Appropriately
for a desert religion, adopted by merchants,

no link between faith and the seasons
was established as each feast arrives
annually a month earlier. But this

lunar, pre-fossil fuel time-table
is comfortless. Even Ibne Mucana,
poet and councillor, our Berber neighbour

a millennium back, even he studied
the gathering swallows as instruction
to prepare his allotment for the rains.

The baffled cicadas that were always invisible,
impossible to track down in their signs,
are doubly inviolate in their silence.

A Footnote on Colonial Bureaucracy
(For Billy Hanafi)

In colonial Morocco,
birth certificates for *sujets*
were all dated Ist January,
the French assuming
wives were impregnated
only on All Fools Day.

In colonial Nyasaland,
Circular B banned
concubinage with *native*
women, so it never
happened and no birth
certificates were signed.

In colonial Angola,
Portuguese men had
free run of the *pretas*,
becoming, so it's written,
uniquely fitted to rule
despite all that paperwork.

These documents, or
their absence, matter
variously for descendants
in the lapsed metropoles
(it's been death back home
for some who showed them).

The Gulf
(For Farid)

1

The man beckoned from behind a trestle
chromed with speakers and ghetto-blasters
(this was '73), his neighbour's stall sweating
with thigh-length platform-heel boots,
another with skin-lighteners and afro-wigs,
and trainers everywhere, ersatz Nike and Adidas,
in a pot-holed main street, lined with kitsch

from three continents. The man beckoned
to the red-faced Englishman, inviting
to a grand tour of his concrete mansion
and indeed, it was a veritable Dubai,
years before the event, a concrete oasis
of walled-in desire, its rampant "Id" spurting
not from black gold but illicit diamonds,

and *in hoc* to *Ideal Home* in the furnishing
of master bedroom and 9 others en suite,
living room, billiard room, bar, smoking room,
kitchen with every electro-processing device
and a garage with four mercedes-benz,
the whole mummified by a laterite dust to
forefinger your initials in, as visitor's book.

I recalled this sadness, over-nighting in Doha,
that Mecca of a religion of sheer money,
with its jewelled palaces and oil-lit skyscrapers,
its tethered palms and struggling petunias,
its migrants sweating under the Emir's portrait,
as the dust clouds blew in from the desert
and the night air was thick with fumes.

2

Which of us hasn't wondered, were we to win
the state lottery, after securing our own and our
family's future, what we'd do for the world?

I'm writing of another Emir, heir to a 300 year
sheikdom, viz. $2,600_2$ kilometers of sand
on the northern fringe of Arabia Felix,

who as a sensitive youth with scholarly tastes,
and the intelligence to back them up, won
the equivalent of a trillion lotteries

when, on his ruling brother's assassination
(while he was writing up his doctoral thesis),
feudal governance fell into his hands

even as those sands erupted in oil. Who
hasn't wondered how our conscience
would cope with unlimited power and riches?

What girls? What palaces? What wine-bearers?
What race-horses, bred to a stable's perfection,
what devotion to the hunt for the perfect pearl?

His first discovery was it was not so. Those
petro-dollars were so much paper until spent,
and nothing constrained like purchase.

Forty years on, that desert bordering
the pearl lagoons is a forest of scyscrapers,
so closely planted the white limousines

are grid bound between neon signs flashing
corporate logos. The scholarly Emir
has fought back with museums of Calligraphy,

of Art, of Heritage, of Archaelogy,
of Natural Science, of Islamic Civilisation,
and 17 others, along with an Aquarium

and 600 mosques, refusing to be swamped
by what he's swamped by, taking time out
as visiting professor at the region's universities,

while the dress and alcohol codes are absolute
in those preposterously luxurious Malls
with their too-big-to-fail franchises.

His second PhD is in Political Science;
his skills are in managing the aristocracy
his desert tribe has become, shutting out

the 73% whose migrant sweat irrigates
this urban desert. Opening the Book Fair,
another of the old man's opposition

projects, his testy speech was an assault
on globalisation, and I wondered which of us
over decades would have done better?

3
Two women in stylish *burkas*, fully
veiled with teasing post-box slits
for window-shopping the Dubai mall,
(one with *Ksubi* shades, completing

the Darth Vader effect), paused at
the entrance to Victoria Secrets,
fingering what even to an old man like me
is the most superfluous of lingerie.

My dear old Ayatollahs, these women
have their secrets, while the 70%
of college students who are female,
their *burkas* their passports, have scented
    your future.
    Why not touch base
    and embrace
    what's on offer?

4

Even hooded, this peregrine falcon
seems preternaturally alert,
though the Falconer assures us
it's bird-brained, without a care
in the world. Even casually
sleeping, it looks a dangerous
machine, its beak hooked
like a claw, its claws biting
into the Falconer's leather-
gloved wrist, its shoulders
packed neat as a parachute,
primed to explode in vertiginous
stooping, out-zagging even
the swallows.
           The hood,
the leather glove and the lure,
were all the Bedouin needed
to recruit these autumn travellers
from Russia to the Congo

in hunting down other
more succulent migrants,
until released to continue
their peregrination south.

                              We've
been spirited to the desert
in a dune-surfing SUV. The sun
blisters my shoulders. The pink
sand, where the wind is already
obliterating our tracks, drifts
to the horizon with not a date
palm's shadow in sight.

                              Unlike
the peregrine's mantle and coverts,
unlike the Bedouin's *keffiyeh*
and *agal*, my shirt and slacks
feel ill-fitting, and I know myself,
for the first time ever, in a place
I could not survive. They knew,
and still know, and I don't – though
our Falconer makes a living
these days among the Emirates'
skyscrapers, breeding hawks
to scare pigeons from luxury malls.

5

It's mankind's story to have drifted
from the forest and veldt
to the farm and now the city,
but no one before has done it
in a single lifetime (nor
skipped the agriculture).

Some, the Irish headmaster said,
keep a caravan to escape to,
by an oasis with a camel
and a dozen date palms,
but in nineteen tours
he's never been invited.

6

The Al Noor Mosque (a.k.a, brightness)
replicates, but chastely, Istambul's
Blue Mosque, itself inspired
by the Hagia Sophia. The roof repeats
the minarets and proud, cascading
domes of the original while the interior,
as with all mosques, is a palace of light,
there being no Gothic mysteries in Islam.

Our hostess wears the inevitable *burka*
but her face is radiant as she explains
the unqualified delights of being Muslim.
The rules could not be simpler, involving
submission for all, and for women modesty.
She laughs, acknowledging the fashions
in *burkas* (her own is cheaply off the shelf),
while men this year are opting for blue.

Even the children are turning sophisticated,
demanding 50 dirham notes for Eid al-Fitr
instead of the 5 of her own childhood.
This is hard for her. But Mohammed
in the Holy Qu'ran (peace be upon him)
says there is no compulsion in religion
and the poor can always offer a smile,
which is her way of trying to be generous.

With each of these smiles, a gulf yawns
between my own and her religion of rules
without paradox or nuance – such as
could explain my outrage no modern Imam
mounts the hundred steps of the minaret
for the pre-dawn Call to Prayer, but kisses
a microphone, source of the clamour
that rattles the windows of my tourist hotel.

7

To economists, souks and shopping malls
are much the same, classified under "retail",
though the souks tend to be "informal sector."

For the rest of us, the gulf could not be wider
between those boulevards of corporate brands
and this stall where a silversmith is hammering

a necklace of intricate design, in a jewellers' alley
of goldsmiths and diamond polishers, alongside
hardware stalls with platters and grills,

spoons and cauldrons on a wedding's scale,
next to fabrics, white calico for the men's tunics,
or the light-blue of today's fashion (or cockroach-

black for *burkas*), or immense bolts of sari silks,
brilliant with sequins, or back-to-back alleys
of carpets and tapestries, or through a tunnel

in this warren of arcades, over-flowing barrels
of almonds, walnuts, pecans and pistaccios,
with boxes of dates and dried apricots, trays

301

of coriander, tumeric, tamarind, cumin,
slithers of cinnamon, clenched cloves, asterisks
of star-anis, green Thai and yellow Habanara

peppers, serranos like scarlet toe-nails,
and dried lemons bouyant as ping-pong balls,
black pepper pellets, rosebuds in scented jars,

a world of odours and textures, colours and tastes
as you proceed into a courtyard of song birds,
mynahs and macaws, budgies and parakeets,

caged like the chameleons and striped iguanas
with rabbits and guinea-pigs, and a coiled python
digesting something still stirring in a corner.

The Mall is a cathedral for the advert-driven
jet-set, the Souk a cornucopia,
an encyclopaedia and a zoo, the one moribund

but all-conquering, the latter vibrant but doomed.

8

Round the Khalid lagoon,
after the dusk Call to Prayer,
after the *kebbe* and aubergines,
they emerge in their thousands
to enjoy the cool night air.

Some wander down on foot,
relaxing on the broad-leaved
savannah grass, some arrive
in limos, taking folding
chairs from the boot;

the men in their tunics
egalitarian, the matriarchs
and the housewives veiled,
the little girls dazzling
in flash-photography silks,

the boys in Wayne Rooney
strip and trainers, hurtling
along the promenade between
the cast-iron lampposts
on scooters and skate boards.

This is one of the sights
of today's world, so many
families contently together
on the well-watered lawns
of the lagoon's five mile circuit

within the encircling concrete
of hotels and shopping malls,
and each mile, the electric–
lit dome of a mosque,
and beyond all the desert.

One exuberant Bedouin kid
in a baseball cap high-fived
this solitary unbeliever
as I sampled the night air,
and I felt privileged.

9

Mohamet was angry. He'd sat through an hour's
multi-cultural wrangling about poetry's
untranslateability (*it's why we do it*),
before questions were coaxed from the floor

and he bounced to his feet, his bearded lips
unfazed by irony. *Arabic*, he avowed, *was
the world's loveliest language. It eclipsed
all others. It was the discourse of paradise.*

*Its poetry had sixteen distinct meters, while
English had merely five. How could its beauties
be rendered in such a* – he was too
courteous to call my dialect vile,

but I saw he saw me as some crude crusader,
some Baldwin or Frederick Barbarossa,
a.k.a. Zuckerberg, Larry Page or Bill Gates,
bringing sacrilege and worse to the Caliphate.

My co-presenter was Tanveer Anjum,
chronicler of Pakistan's most desolate children,
("What will you do when you're grown up?"
"I am grown up. I can make a bomb").

She demanded dialectical equality, but
neither Chomsky, nor the sheer power
of her translated images, impressed Mohamet,
whose tired expression had lived it all before.

Poetry on the Underground

A blind man taps the whole length
of the metro platform, clicking
every few paces the corrugated strip
dyed a yellow he cannot see,
beyond which, a metre down,
is humming certain death.

His unseeing gaze is horizontal,
no childhood memory making him
glance down at danger, till
just before the rising escalator
he makes a military turn
sharp right, and waits

precisely where the front
door of the train's first
carriage lurches open with a hiss,
and he steps aboard,
to resume what he does
all weekdays daily, tapping

the train's whole length
as it plunges through tunnels
mapped in his pulsing wrist
so each shopping mall
of a station finds him
opposite a train door begging.

Over the years, I've ridden
the metro with him, always
clicking a coin in his box.
He can't possibly know me

yet I'm convinced he does,
witnessing everything

from his mole's vantage
point, who's off where
in our surface skirmishing,
on what business or
assignation, our arrivals
endlessly postponed.

It's the line's strict discipline
this Teresias is versed in
with his eloquent tapping,
a metre from sure death,
leaving me spellbound
by this brush with myth.

Still Among the Living

This elderly, black optician
with the broad, glistening dome,
all we can see as he inscribes
our names on the official form
testifying, for licence purposes,
we're still among the living
with eyesight adequate for driving,

hails from the Dominican Republic,
free Haiti's doppel-gänger,
and employs the calligraphy
he was taught in the convent,
as practised when his forebears

were slaves of imperial Spain.
He brings this monk's talent

to a provincial town in Portugal
where the bureaucracy's not
so different. Who cares whether
we can see or not? The bribe
is merely customary. Our papers
are rubber stamped, their
copperplate irrefutable.

The Weightier Craft

So the Market won
when the Berlin Wall came down?
"It's OK," said the jumping Banker,
"I landed on a Tax Payer."

Every stone in this dry stone wall
the post-equinoctial sun is exploring
was individually weighed and chiselled
and contoured, neat as a jigsaw,
by a smiling immigrant from Bulgaria,
prepared, now other walls have fallen,
to work for less pay than the locals
in a craft in which we're no longer skilled.

Dry stone walls are ubiquitous here,
tiny abandoned plots and folds
cleared over centuries of the stones
they're assembled of. They huddle,
marking ever shrinking boundaries
as the land was divided, the consolidating

alliance eaten by fresh dowries
and inheritance-hungry sons, until

all the country is fit for are onions
and wall-hurdling goats. Driving
past, I often stop and covet them,
practicing my lichenometry, wondering
at lives made ever more confined
by clinging, at such endless labour
ended at last by flight to America
or to France as the city, encroaching

with bulldozers, spreads suburb and shanty
to the outskirts of the next town.
As always, I am at odds with history.
Hating walls, I have commissioned one
from a local builder, who exploits
this smiling Bulgarian with the old skills.
There's no anachronism in money spent
making my peace with a past so recent,

for the queue of cars, held up by a tractor
en route to the motorway slip road,
the 3-pronged hoe and 4 by 4 Range Rover,
inhabit the same historical moment
as immigrant replaces emigrant,
and the tyranny of old production modes
floats free as a dandelion of goods and services
in our too-big-to-fail Las Vegas.

Our metaphors for what's most valued,
what's most of worth or held most dear
in our base-forged commonwealth
are socially minted. If the coinage fails,

if the poems are mere fiduciary paper,
derivatives or default swaps,
let hunting, gathering and barter
re-invent the speech of a stone-age fire.

The stones our mason has set in place,
their colours x-rayed by the leaning sun,
fossils that once hissed and bubbled
millennia before humans appeared,
will outlive any poem of mine,
his craft weightier and untroubled
by such anxieties, even as I tuck
a ten euro note in his shirt pocket.

Where Transparency's the Buzz Word

Hans Andersen's delicious satire
The Emperor's New Clothes
has an ending hitherto undisclosed,
revealed by his translator

in the English version she prepared
(rejected by her publisher).
Hans told her on his British tour
that the little boy who gushed

"Crickey! The Emperor's naked!"
was upbraided by the spectators
for ruining the royal parade,
and beaten with walking sticks.

This is so what would happen
in celebrity-driven London.

Now nakedness is the fashion,
the moral's turned upsidedown.

Imagine that tailor's catwalk,
in Paris, New York or Milan,
his swans anorexic ducklings,
his guests known for being known,

the boy, the Emperor and Hans,
all three beyond the pale,
cherishing the old fairy tale
that once had resonance.

I Live Once Again where People are Without Hope

This is different from those villages where
the women's songs anticipate a recap
of the present, that the rains will be there

when prayed for, and that of a mixed crop
requiring different states of weather,
some will be harvested. If war disrupts

the planting season, or if the ancestors
withhold the rains, if the children take
to the bush with cutlasses, reaping a harvest

of death, there is no comfort in thinking
of possible futures. Only the past
brings any calmness of mind. It's unlike

here, where time's linear, and people
had become used to hope. Disaster
could always strike, but the trope

had lost its link with the seven planets.
Absolutism had finally been rejected
in an amiable revolution, with even the priests

embracing the utopian dialectic
of one person one vote. All the rules
of the game were rehearsed in a politics

of fixed-term parliaments, trade unions, schools
for all, and a free press, with the rich
no longer ancestrally in control,

and all's come to nothing. Debates, marches,
slogans, general strikes, snap elections,
even talk of a further military putsch,

have exhausted all the traditional options.
There remains this counter-Byzantium,
Portugalia geriatrica, the dying generations

of pensioners in one another's arms:
no begetting or birth
in a country of retirement homes,

and the culture's slow death.

In Praise of the Lyric

Gentle troubadours
had no desire for conquest
other than women.

Drumming up crusades
was never their ambition,
too Arab for that.

As for the epic,
those battles were dead and gone,
the line established.

In the scented dusk,
a lute, a.k.a. guitar,
the weapon of choice,

and a balcony,
a woman in lingerie,
approached from below.

As metaphor, no
arma virumque cano
ever expressed more.

Pastoral

1

No one who's courted a maize patch through
hoeing, planting, watering, weeding
and gathering the improbable cobs, could ever
have been a Surrealist, teasing the bourgeosie
with the adolescent aim of driving them crazy.

No one who's folded compost into a plot
for onions, peppers, parsnips, aubergine
and the rest, as they duplicate themselves
so accurately below and above ground,
could have embraced the Modernist wasteland.

No one who's fought off slugs and aphids,
blight and fungi, fruit fly and mole-crickets,
to reap such delights of vegetable flesh,
could, in whatever fit of urban disillusion,
have swallowed Post-Modernist Deconstruction.

Poetry lost its way when it migrated to cities
with their linear trends, their harvests
endlessly postponed. It spurns manifestos.
it eludes the clutch of theorists. It germinates,
like these okra seeds I never thought would shoot.

2

But the twentieth was the century of migration
to the shanty-towns of Kingston and Nairobi,
the *banlieues* of Paris, the inner-London boroughs,

and they have their own poetry of violent
self-assertion, their amplified rhymes spat
across barricades of revolving strobe lights

into a gloom of ethnic and gendered identity,
and who can blame them, when our own kids,
the ones baffled by Jamie's classroom onion,

are intoxicated with them as role models?
Poetry must pick its own way through the din,
googling its maculate descent from riddles.

Game Park Fable

After a pre-dawn drive, we saw
across a mist-bound valley
elephants herding, walking
on clouds, their gentle
trunks swaying as though
scenting where a path might be.

First light too, the molasses-
barge engine clearing
its oily throat as minature
perfect crocodiles
slid from the decks
to melt into the slipstream;

or the mahogany tree
glimpsed from the diesel's
window, silhouetted
against silver, its strange
fruit a troupe of monkeys
as yet barely stirring.

Dawn was what Union Jacks
lowered at midnight
were all about. Fifty
years on, the sun
seems roped backwards
struggling to rise,

as the crocodiles reign
supreme, and the tree-
bound monkeys scratch
their fleas, while those
gently strolling giants
seem pacing to extinction.

Lisbon & London

Leaving the cafe, I follow a cobbled track
past a row of clay-and wattle cottages
that haven't seen white-wash in decades,
past a tiny park with ancient acacias
dangling their seedy black pods, past
a peeling hoarding and a tennis court
doubling as a 7-a-side football pitch,
the whole shut in between 16-floor tower-
blocks, their verandas draped with washing,
built at odd angles, as though obeying
some ancient division of this manor
of which these cobbles are all that remain.

Bits of any city are like this. It takes
centuries or world wars to obliterate
centuries, and even then you'll encounter
some flight of marble steps to nowhere,
and a god-knows how old *oliveira*,

or indigo jacaranda or a stunted yew,
in their determined latitudes. But only
in London do you stumble on burial grounds,
Crossbones, Nunhead, Woodgrange, Margravine,
Bunhill Fields, hallowed by Bunyan and Blake,
Highgate, with George Eliot and Marx,
the closest grave to the latter a Landeg's.

Tattoo
(to the sound of Greek bagpipes)

Today, the Greek Government
executed by firing squad
1000 pensioners, along
with 2000 workers, as part
of a package of financial
reforms, to reassure
the markets and permit
the Troika to release one
more tranche of the bail-out.

How one feels for the victims
In all this, the bankers
criminalised, shorn
of bonuses, the markets
bearish, nervous as
kittens, the green back,
the pound, the tsunami–
floating yen, scurrying
between time-sealed

vaults and tax-havens,
exposed to the sniping

of credit default swaps
as Molotov cocktails
rain down relentlessly
from Fitch's, Moody's,
and S.& P.'s. Will
the friendly Troika
contrive fresh reforms?

Will our young friend,
the euro, be vaporised?
Growth is a must come
what may, be it 3000
health workers hung,
drawn and quartered,
4000 firemen burned
at the stake, even
the odd politician garrotted.

Six Decades On

Harvest Festivals, in Glasgow or Birkenhead,
were the only chapel services I didn't sleep
through as a child. The congregation sang earnestly
of ploughing, scattering the good seed, and reaping,
sheer metaphor to men from soot-encrusted
tenements or Cammel Laird's shipyards,
and sermonised as such from my father's pulpit

yet strangely meaningful, while four sheaves
of wheat (where did they get them?) clasping
that pulpit in pastoral parenthesis, presided over
a communion table of tinned tomatoes, tinned
mandarin oranges and spam, sliced-bread

in greaseproof wrappers, sour bunches of grapes,
destined for the Old Peoples' Home, all metaphors

in turn for an endlessly receding metaphor
like the Gordon Highlander and Sikh orderly
in the Camp Coffee label. But I, not long before,
from my perch in the lime tree by the garden fence,
had watched Clydesdales stamping at the furrow's
end, turning for the next couplet as John Clare's
heir apparent took fresh aim at the horizon.

That was briefly an England shorn of metal, as
lamp posts and park railings were recycled
as Spitfires, as cornfields bled with poppies
and the handcut wheat was stacked in sheaves,
with gleaners bowed like Biblical Ruth. It was over
in an instant, this glimpse of the land before
The Deserted Village, even as pony-drawn carts

delivered milk to your doorstep, and dray-horses
hauled sacks of coal. Then humming milk floats
heralded peace, and anthracite for the winter of '47
was shouldered from shuddering lorries. But I'd
glimpsed, amid the undisclosed holocaust, a spool
of innocence, when ploughman's sweat basted
the earth and the harvest metaphor was actual.

Where I live decades on, men stride the cobbled
square as though crossing ploughed fields, and what
their wives are marketing was harvested at dawn.
The tomatoes we raise in their due season,
aubergines, sweet pepper, walnuts and quince,
and ferry in reed baskets to city friends who
uncork red wine in response, feel sacramental.

Acknowledgements

Acknowledgements are due to the editors of *325, Kunapipi, Mau* (Malawi), *Moving Worlds, Odi* (Malawi), *Poetry Review, Poetry Wales*, *Planet*, *Southern African Review of Books, Stand, Thames Poetry, The Independent, The Times Literary Supplement*, *The Warwick Review*, the *1985 Anthology of the Avon Poetry Competition*, and *A Talent(ed) Digger* (ed. Maes-Jelinek, Collier & Davis), in which some of these poems first appeared. 'Bacalhau', 'The Three Graces' and 'October's Sickle Moon' were first published in Portuguese in *Superfícies e Interiores: Poemas de Landeg White* (Introdução, Selecção, Tradução e Notas de Hélio Osvaldo Alves, CEMAR 1995).

For Captain Stedman: Poems was published by Harry Chambers/Peterloo Poets (1983), *The View from the Stockade* and *Bounty* by Dangaroo Press (1991 & 1993), *South* and *Travellers Palm* by CEMAR (Figueira da Foz, Portugal, 1999 & 2001), and *Where the Angolans are Playing Football: Selected and New Poems*, *Arab Work*, and *Singing Bass* by Parthian (2003, 2006 & 2009).

For *Bounty*, my principal sources are O Rutter (ed.), *The Trial of the Bounty Mutineers* (Edinburgh, 1931), Douglas L. Oliver, *Ancient Tahitian Society*, 3 vol. (University of Hawaii Press, 1974), and Lt. Wm. Bligh, *The Log of HMS Bounty 1787-89* (Guildford: Genesis publications, 1975). Oliver quotes three different traditions for the origins of Oro, the youngest of the gods. I have followed the third.

The opening and closing sections are adapted from Hugh Carrington (ed.), *The Discovery of Tahiti: a Journal of the Second Voyage of HMS Dolphin ... written by her master George Robertson* (The Hakluyt Society, 2nd series, no. XLVIII, 1948) and Charles Darwin, *The Voyage of the Beagle* (Dent, 1959).